22

60

106

Contents

4-5	What's on the box?
6-7	Airfix Social Media
8	Aerodrome
9	Workbench
10-19	Airfix QUICKBUILD
20-31	Starter Sets
	Small Starter Sets
	Medium Starter Sets
	Large Starter Sets
32-35	Gift Sets
36-37	RMS Titanic Sets
38-69	Military Aircraft
	1:72 Scale
	1:48 Scale
	1:24 Scale
70-73	Military Vehicles
74-75	Ruined Buildings
76-91	Vintage Classic Sets
	Aircraft
	Military Vehicless
	D Day Tanks
	Military Figures
	Ships
92	Space
93	RNLI
93	Engineer
94	Board Game
95-105	Technical Index
106-127	Humbrol

www.airfix.com

WHAT'S ON THE BOX

WHAT'S ON THE BOX

Airfix kits are available in three types: **Starter Sets**, **Gift Sets** and **Classics**. Every kit box contains a wealth of information to help you choose the best kit and achieve the best finish.

Starter Sets

Are ideal for beginners and include glue, paint and brushes with one finish option.

Gift Sets

Are ideal for more advanced modellers and include glue, paint and brushes.

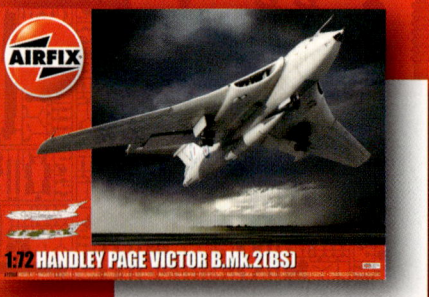

Classic Kits

A kit on its own without glue, paint and brushes. Available in multiple finish options depending on the kit series.

Vintage Classics

Enjoy the nostalgia with our revival of classic models. The boxes feature original paintings by an impressive range of artists.

www.airfix.com

1. History
A small piece of history is included on the top of each Airfix kit box. This gives some background information of the product, including actions the real item was involved in. The area also shows the dimensions of the finished model and the number of pieces.

2. Flying hours
Become a member of the Airfix Club and you can collect the Flying Hours to receive FREE model kits. The bigger the kit, the more Flying Hours are available to accumulate.

3. Skill level
The skill level, from 1 to 4, explains how difficult the model will be. A higher skill level kit often has more parts and is more challenging to build.

4. Paint list
The paint list shows and explains the recommended list of Humbrol™ paints that will enable you to create the best finish for your model. (Please note, this area is on Classic kits only. A full list of Humbrol™ paints required are in the kit instructions for larger Gift Sets).

5. Schemes
The scheme options are outlined on the top of the box to show how many choices of scheme are available, with their markings and descriptions.

6. Decals
The side profiles on the front show how many decal options are possible and what they will look like.

7. Product code
The product code is unique to each kit. It helps you to identify your kit of choice easily, assists with navigating through the catalogue or Airfix website accurately, determines the size of the kit and gives guidance to the number of parts. The Classic Kit product code also helps you to understand the size of the model via the Series system. The kit Series starts at 1 through to 25 (the higher the number, the larger the kit). The first two digits after the "A" determine the Series of the kit. The example product code here, A06016 is Series 6.

8. Model scales
The scale of the kit indicates how large the model will be in relation to the full size. A 1:72 scale kit therefore is 72x smaller than the original (1:48 = 48x smaller). The smaller the scale number – eg 1:24 = the larger the kit compared to the original.

1:72   1:48   1:24

www.airfix.com

SOCIAL MEDIA

facebook.com/OfficialAirfix

twitter.com/Airfix

youtube.com/OfficialAirfix

instagram.com/OfficialAirfix

airfix.com/forum

www.airfix.com

Connect with AIRFIX fans worldwide

- Build your skill, understanding and friendship – at the same time as building your model!
- Join thousands of people with the same passion
- Gain a wealth of historical knowledge
- Get up-to-the-minute offer and event information
- Frequent competitions and prizes
- Share your skills with others
- Tips and techniques videos

#WorkspaceWednesday

- Don't forget to head over to Facebook or Twitter to share your #WorkspaceWednesday pictures with us.

Whether you are embarking on your first Airfix model, or are a master builder, joining our online communities will help you take the experience even further. Airfix social networking is the fastest and most informed way to find out about the hobby, latest events, special offers and competitions.

Our communities are formed of like-minded people keen to share tips and ideas, so you can get the most from this exciting and absorbing hobby. Online you will find forums, blogs and YouTube technique videos, whilst our Tweets alert you to offers, with Facebook keeping you abreast of all things Airfix and Humbrol.

So if you're not already part of our community why not **join in**?

www.airfix.com

AERODROME

Aviation enthusiasts cleared for take-off with Aerodrome.

Aeroplanes are the most exciting machines produced by man and have been a source of fascination since the Wright Brothers made their first successful manned, powered flight in 1903. Through two world wars, into the jet age and beyond, aeroplanes have always been at the cutting edge of technology and continue to enthral and inspire to this day – designed by geniuses, flown by heroes.

Our Aerodrome blog is produced with a love of all things aviation at its heart and is published in the community section of both the Airfix and Corgi websites. It is an indulgence in the subject of aviation and includes reports from Airshows and Museums, special aviation related events around the UK and regularly features historic articles from our extensive archives. Whether reporting from the atmospheric surroundings of the Great War airfield at Stow Maries, or bringing you the thrill of the flying action from the latest Royal International Air Tattoo, Aerodrome is the blog where aviation enthusiasts come together to share their passion for aviation.

http://www.airfix.com/aerodrome

AIRFIX WORKBENCH

Would you like to find out all the very latest news from the Airfix development team including new tooling announcements and modelling exclusives? If the answer is yes, you need to join the thousands of modelling enthusiasts all over the world who regularly read our Airfix Workbench blog, which is published every two weeks on the community section of Airfix website and now one of our most popular publications.

Providing readers with a fascinating insight behind the scenes at Airfix, Workbench is proud to bring our readers the very latest information and updates from the most eagerly anticipated new tooling projects and is full of exclusive content, reader supplied articles and interesting modelling related features. If you want to be the first to find out about new model tooling announcements or see the latest box artwork reveals before anyone else, then Airfix Workbench is the blog for you.

There is an interesting story behind every one of the kits featured in the Airfix model range and our Workbench blog is the place where you can discover everything you need to know.

http://www.airfix.com/workbench

AIRFIX QUICKBUILD

QUICKBUILD

No paint required
just decorate with stickers

- Pre-Coloured
- Stickers Provided
- Push Fit
- Age 5+

Push together
each kit has between 27 and 52 parts

Please visit **www.airfix.com/catalogue2019** to locate your nearest Airfix QUICKBUILD stockist

No glue!
No paint!
Just BUILD!

coming SOON

Coming later in 2019
ALL New Models

We are happy to announce six exciting new models for 2019. Compatible with other major plastic building block brands, QuickBuild is the easy way to 'quickly build' detailed and accurate models!

- Jaguar i-Pace E-Trophy
- Audi TT
- Bugatti Chiron
- Ford F-150
- F-35 Lightning II
- Ford Mustang GT

AIRFIX QUICKBUILD

www.airfix.co.uk/quickbuild

AIRFIX QUICKBUILD

VW Camper Van red

Available Now — Code: **J6017**

VW Camper Van blue

Available Now — Code: **J6024**

VW Beetle yellow

Available Now — Code: **J6023**

Please visit www.airfix.com/catalogue2019 to locate your nearest Airfix QUICKBUILD stockist

NEW

VW Camper Van 'Surfin''

Available June-19 — Code: **J6032**

NEW

VW Beetle 'Flower Power'

Available June-19 — Code: **J6031**

AIRFIX QUICKBUILD

www.airfix.co.uk/quickbuild

AIRFIX QUICKBUILD

Lamborghini Aventador white

Available Now　　　Code: **J6019**

Bugatti Veyron 16.4 black/red

Available Now　　　Code: **J6020**

McLaren P1™ green

Available Now　　　Code: **J6021**

Please visit www.airfix.com/catalogue2019 to locate your nearest Airfix QUICKBUILD stockist

NEW

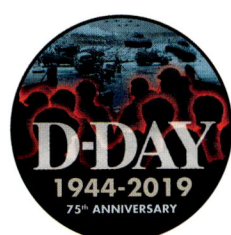

D-Day Spitfire

NEW

Available April-19 Code: **J6045**

NEW

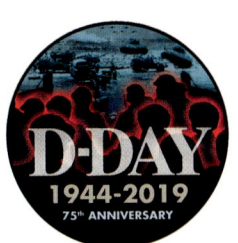

D-Day P-51D Mustang™

Available April-19 Code: **J6046**

AIRFIX QUICKBUILD

www.airfix.co.uk/quickbuild

AIRFIX QUICKBUILD

Spitfire

Available Now — Code: **J6000**

Messerschmitt Bf109

Available Now — Code: **J6001**

P-51D Mustang™

Available Now — Code: **J6016**

Please visit www.airfix.com/catalogue2019 to locate your nearest Airfix QUICKBUILD stockist

Red Arrows Hawk

ROYAL AIR FORCE **RED ARROWS**

Available Now — Code: **J6018**

BAE Hawk

Available Now — Code: **J6003**

www.airfix.co.uk/quickbuild

AIRFIX QUICKBUILD

Eurofighter Typhoon

Available Now — Code: **J6002**

F-22®Raptor®

Available Now — Code: **J6005**

Harrier

Available Now — Code: **J6009**

Please visit www.airfix.com/catalogue2019 to locate your nearest Airfix QUICKBUILD stockist

Apache™

AH-64 APACHE LONGBOW™

Available Now — Code: **J6004**

Challenger Tank

Available Now — Code: **J6010**

Challenger Tank

Available Now — Code: **J6022**

www.airfix.co.uk/quickbuild

AIRFIX QUICKBUILD

STARTER SETS

From Starter Sets for the beginner to more elaborate Gift Sets, the following pages have something for everyone.

A brilliant way to start the fantastic hobby of Airfix modelling!

Starter Sets all contain paint, adhesive and brushes.

Please visit www.airfix.com/catalogue2019 to locate your nearest Airfix stockist

STARTER SETS

www.airfix.com

SMALL STARTER SETS

A series of iconic aircraft, tank and ship models for the beginner. Sets include glue, brush and four acrylic paints – all that's needed to complete a fabulous first kit!

RE-INTRODUCION Mary Rose

Mary Rose

1:400 Available March-19 Code: **A55114**

Famous as the only Tudor era war ship preserved anywhere in the world, the Mary Rose was a Carrack type vessel that served for many years before her final action on the 19th of July 1545. The wreck lay undiscovered and undisturbed for hundreds of years before being rediscovered in 1971 and raised back to the surface in 1982. Today preserved by the Mary Rose Trust in the museum in Portsmouth, the ship now stands as a great testament to the life of a Tudor sailor.

Please visit www.airfix.com/catalogue2019 to locate your nearest Airfix stockist

NEW Willys MB Jeep®

Willys MB Jeep®

1:72

The Willys MB Jeep®, officially designated Truck, ½-ton, 4x4, is the best known of all the American vehicles of the Second World War. Originally intended to be a command and reconnaissance car, it became the most versatile of all vehicles. Able to be armed with machine guns and to tow small artillery pieces, the Jeep® was essential to the Allied war effort.

Available May-19 **Code: A55117**

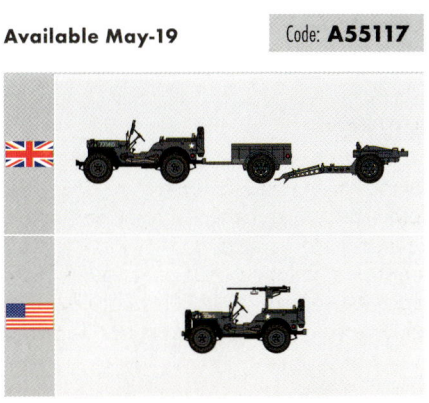

SMALL STARTER SETS

www.airfix.com

SMALL STARTER SETS

Aircraft Display Stands — Code: AF1008

Containing an assortment of clear display stands for single aircraft. There are three sizes of stands suited to 1:72 scale models. This assortment enables a whole squadron of aircraft to be displayed.

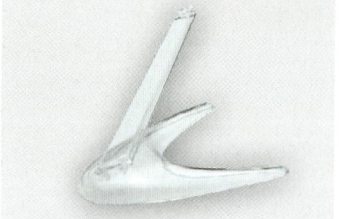

Available Now

 1:72

Supermarine Spitfire Mk.Ia — Code: A55100

Probably the best known fighter aircraft ever, and arguably the best looking too, with its sleek lines and elliptical wings, the Spitfire will be forever remembered for its role in the Battle of Britain.

Available Now

Curtiss Tomahawk IIB — Code: A55101

The Tomahawk was used extensively throughout WWII. The shark-mouth version in this set is one of the most famous looking aircraft of the period, making it great fun to build.

Available Now

HMS Victory — Code: A55104

Probably the most famous warship ever, HMS Victory is still to be seen in Portsmouth Dockyard. This great miniature model is a fun way to start modelling.

Available Now

RAF Red Arrows Gnat — Code: A55105

The Royal Air Force Aerobatic Team (RAFAT), the formal name of the Red Arrows, began life at RAF Fairford, Gloucestershire in 1965. Initially there were seven display pilots and ten Gnat jet trainers. The name 'Red Arrows' was chosen to combine the appeal and expertise of two earlier teams, the Black Arrows and the Red Pelicans.

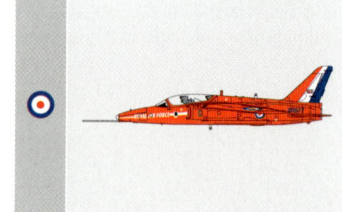

Available Now

 1:72

Messerschmitt Bf109E-3 — Code: A55106

The Bf109E-3 was one of the first true fighters of the modern era and was the Luftwaffe's main bomber escort during the Battle of Britain. After some spectacular successes at the beginning of the war it found its main challengers to be the RAF's Hurricane and Spitfire.

Available Now

Please visit www.airfix.com/catalogue2019 to locate your nearest Airfix stockist

Hunting Percival Jet Provost T.4

Code: **A55116A**

The highly successful Jet Provost provided the RAF with a training solution for over thirty years. During this period, many RAF stations operated aerobatic display teams and the Central Flying School's 'Red Pelicans' were amongst the most distinctive, often flying in the same display programme as the Red Arrows.

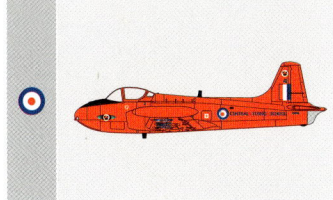

Available Now

North American Mustang Mk.IV™

Code: **A55107**

The Mustang came into its own when fitted with the Merlin engine. Its long range enabled it to escort bombers deep into enemy territory. The Royal Air Force flew the type from 1944 onwards in support of Bomber Command's long distance raids deep into enemy territory.

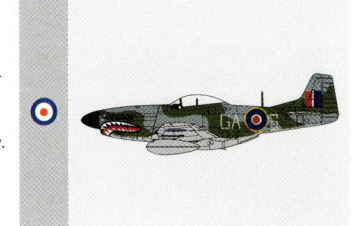

Available Now

Cromwell Mk.IV

Code: **A55109**

The agile and reliable Cromwell Mk.IV tank made its operational debut in Normandy 1944. It soon made its mark on the battlefield and became one of the most successful tanks of the British Army.

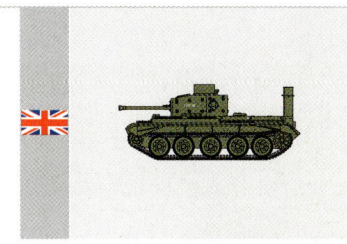

Available Now

Focke Wulf FW190A-8

Code: **A55110**

The feared Focke Wulf 190A-8 was the most numerous of the classic Luftwaffe fighter, with over 6,655 A-8 produced. Due to constant attacks by allied bombers this type was manufactured by at least eight factories during its lifetime.

Available Now

Hawker Hurricane Mk.I

Code: **A55111**

One of the greatest fighter aircraft of WWII, this version fought alongside the Spitfire and actually shot down and destroyed more aircraft during the Battle of Britain in the summer of 1940 than its even more famous partner!

Available Now

Multipose WWII German Infantry Figures

Code: **A55210**

WWII German Infantry were easily identifiable by their grey uniforms and distinctive coal scuttle helmets, they were often armed with either Mauser rifles or MP40 submachine guns.

Available Now

SMALL STARTER SETS

www.airfix.com

MEDIUM STARTER SETS

These contain more iconic aircraft and vehicles, but this range's models are a little more challenging to build with more parts, 6 paints and 2 brushes.

Aston Martin DB5 Silver — Code: **A50089A**

The DB5 had a new tail design, offering improved aerodynamics. Options now included power steering (on MK1 cars), air conditioning, automatic transmission, limited slip differential and a 325bhp Vantage engine.

Available Now

Jaguar E-Type — Code: **A55200**

Described by Enzo Ferrari as the most beautiful car ever made upon its unveiling, the Jaguar E-type has gone on to become one of the most instantly recognisable and iconic shapes in automotive history.

Available Now

Triumph Herald — Code: **A55201**

The Triumph Herald was a small two-door car introduced in 1959 by the Standard-Triumph Company of Coventry. The body design was by the Italian stylist Michelotti and total Herald sales numbered well over 300,000.

Available Now

VW Beetle — Code: **A55207**

The civil production of the Beetle started in December 1945 and only finished in 2003. Originally powered by a 1100cc air-cooled four cylinder engine, it was continually updated throughout the Beetle's history, culminating in the 1584cc engine found in the final Mexican variants.

Available Now

Douglas A-4B Skyhawk™ — Code: **A55203**

The Douglas A-4 Skyhawk is a carrier-capable ground-attack aircraft designed for the United States Navy and United States Marine Corps. Skyhawks were the Navy's primary light bomber used over North Vietnam during the early years of the Vietnam War.

Available Now

RAF Red Arrows Hawk
Code: **A55202C**

The dual control BAE Hawk T. Mk.1 is the RAF's advanced trainer and has been used by the Red Arrows since 1979. The aircraft is essentially the same as those aircraft flown by the Royal Air Force's 100 Squadron with the exception of the smoke generators and a slightly uprated engine giving a faster response time to changes of power setting.

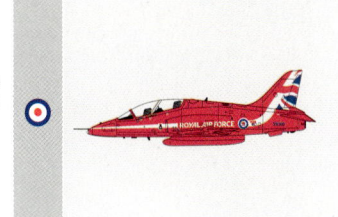

Available Now

de Havilland Vampire T.11
Code: **A55204**

As a two-seater trainer, the Vampire T11 excelled. The side by side seating ensured both pilots had good visibility. The aircraft's inherent stability and docility also made it a relatively safe and effective platform for instruction.

Available Now

Hawker Harrier GR.1
Code: **A55205**

Known affectionally as the "Jump Jet" the Harrier GR1 was the first vertical take-off and landing aircraft flown operationally by the RAF, coming into service in 1969. It soon became a crowd favourite, drawing huge crowds whenever it was putting on its unique display.

Available Now

Hawker Typhoon Mk.Ib
Code: **A55208**

Designed initially to replace the Hawker Hurricane as the complementary high-altitude fighter to the Supermarine Spitfire, the Typhoon instead found its fame as a low altitude ground attack aircraft, spearheading the airborne assault through occupied Europe after D-Day.

Available Now

Boulton Paul Defiant Mk.I
Code: **A55213**

The Boulton Paul Defiant was designed and built by Boulton Paul Aircraft as a "turret fighter" without any forward firing guns and served as an interceptor aircraft with the RAF during the Second World War. Often maligned as a failure, it found a niche as a night fighter during the Blitz.

Available Now

Grumman F4F-4 Wildcat™
Code: **A55214**

The Grumman F4F Wildcat was an American carrier-based fighter aircraft that began service with both the United States Navy and the British Royal Navy with high air combat kill-to-loss ratios. The Wildcat was built throughout the war to serve on escort carriers where larger and heavier fighters could not be used.

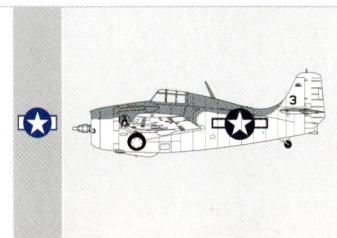

Available Now

MEDIUM STARTER SETS

www.airfix.com

LARGE STARTER SETS

If modern jets, helicopters or cars are your thing, then these sets are perfect for gifts or to build yourself once you've mastered the basics.

1:72 RE-INTRODUCTION

Panavia Tornado F.3

The Tornado F.3 was the RAF's dedicated interceptor fighter. It had a longer fuselage than it's sister GR4, which permitted greater internal fuel stowage. An important feature of the F3 was its ability to patrol at long distance from its base, supported by air-to-air refuelling.

Available June-19

Code: **A55301**

1:72 NEW SCHEME RE-INTRODUCTION

McDonnell Douglas™ F-15A Eagle™

Code: **A55311**

One of the truly great combat aircraft of the post war era, the McDonnell Douglas F-15A was a single seat, all weather air superiority fighter, which at the time, was one of the most expensive military programmes in history. Designed around the fighter pilot with the intention of producing an aircraft which would allow him to dominate the battlefield, the F-15 was known as the 'Ultimate MiG slayer', as it provided the USAF with a fighter which was without equal in the world's skies and became the aircraft against which all future fighter designs would be judged. Despite being in service for more than forty years, the F-15 is still a formidable combat aircraft and is even being considered for further upgrade to keep it in front line service for many years to come.

Available June-19

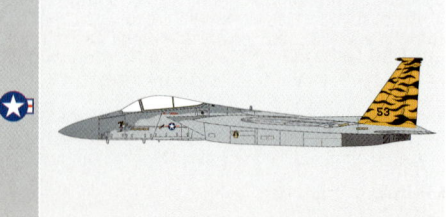

Please visit www.airfix.com/catalogue2019 to locate your nearest Airfix stockist

General Dynamics F-16A® Fighting Falcon®

`Code: A55312`

Designed in the aftermath of the Vietnam War and the need to equip the USAF with a dominant air superiority fighter, the General Dynamics F-16 Fighting Falcon was the first aircraft intentionally designed to be aerodynamically unstable, making this an extremely manoeuvrable aircraft, but one relying heavily on computer controlled fly-by-wire technology. Introduced in 1978, the F-16 is still in service today with several of the world's air arms and has become the most heavily produced modern Western jet fighter in history, serving not only in the US Air Force, but also with 25 overseas nations. This striking aircraft has become famous as the mount of the USAF Air Demonstration Squadron 'Thunderbirds', who have operated the F-16 since the 1983 display season.

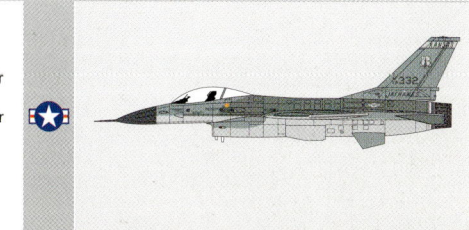

Available June-19

McDonnell Douglas™ F-18A Hornet™

`Code: A55313`

As the US Air Force upgraded their fighter capability with the introduction of the F-15 Eagle and F-16 Fighting Falcon, the US Navy and Marine Corps were looking for a new aircraft to fulfil the dual roles of fleet defender and strike platform. The resultant aircraft was another American jet classic, the McDonnell Douglas F-18 Hornet, a distinctive looking twin engined fighter which provided naval units with a significant capability upgrade. Required to operate in the demanding environment of aircraft carriers at sea, the Hornet is an extremely tough aeroplane and has proved to be effective in the roles for which it was originally intended and flexible enough to take on additional duties. Also proving itself effective and reliable in combat, the Hornet is perhaps best known as the aircraft operated by the US Navy Flight Demonstration Squadron, the 'Blue Angels', with the team flying the F-18 since November 1986. The team are regarded as one of the premier aerobatic display teams in the world and their thrilling displays of precision flying are the highlight of any Airshow in which they perform.

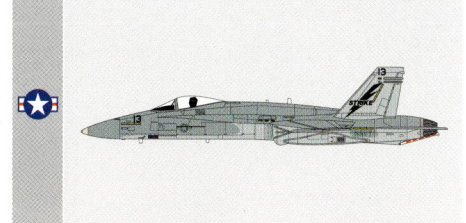

Available June-19

LARGE STARTER SETS

www.airfix.com

LARGE STARTER SETS

1:76

King Tiger Tank

Code: **A55303**

The King Tiger (Tiger II) was a 68 ton monster appearing on the battlefield in 1944. Had the numbers supplied been larger and the fuel to run them been available then the war may have gone on longer than it did.

MEDIUM STARTER SET

Available Now

1:72

Eurofighter Typhoon

Code: **A50098**

The Eurofighter Typhoon is Europe's premier swing role fighter jet. Designed and constructed by a consortium of companies under contract to the United Kingdom, Germany, Italy and Spain. The RAF declared it combat ready in 2006.

Available Now

1:72

BAE Harrier GR.9A

Code: **A55300**

Flown by the Joint Force Harrier Squadrons crewed by both Royal Navy and RAF crews, this ultimate Harrier carried a vast array of weapons, communications and systems to carry offensive operations to the enemy both from land and sea.

Available Now

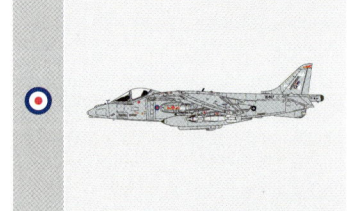

1:72

English Electric Lightning F.2A

Code: **A55305**

The English Electric Lightning was a supersonic jet fighter aircraft of the Cold War era, noted for its great speed. It is the only all-British Mach 2 fighter aircraft and was the first aircraft in the world capable of cruising at Mach+ speeds. It could carry the awesome Firestreak missile.

Available Now

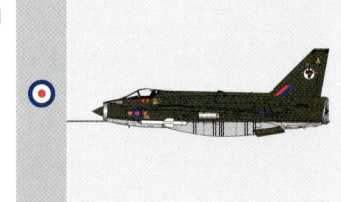

1:72

Westland Sea King HAR.3

Held in extremely high regard by the British public, the distinctive yellow Search and Rescue Sea King HAR.3 helicopters of the Royal Air Force always seemed to be on hand when help was needed most. Many sailors, climbers and holidaymakers owe their lives to the highly capable SAR crews of the RAF.

Available Now

Code: **A55307A**

Please visit www.airfix.com/catalogue2019 to locate your nearest Airfix stockist

Aston Martin DBR9
Code: **A50110**

The Gulf Aston Martin DBR9s performed superbly at Le Mans 2008. Car 009, driven by David Brabham, Antonio García and Darren Turner, won the GT1 class. The 007 car, with Heinz-Harald Frentzen, Andrea Piccini and Karl Wendlinger finished fourth.

Available Now

Ford Fiesta WRC
Code: **A55302**

Developed from the standard road car, this bespoke rally car was built by M-Sport for the works Ford Rally Team for use in the World Rally Championship.

Available Now

MINI Countryman WRC
Code: **A55304**

The MINI Countryman is a 4x4 powered by a 1.6-litre turbocharged engine. Rally aces Prodrive, who masterminded Colin McRae and Richard Burns' championship-winning campaigns, prepared the Countryman. Prodrive also build MINI WRCs for privateers.

Available Now

Jaguar XKR GT3
Code: **A55306**

Jaguar created many fantasy schemes for the XKR GT3 and this is one such official scheme that will really make this fantastic car stand out.

Available Now

Ford 3 Litre GT
Code: **A55308**

Capable of reaching incredible top speeds of well over 350 km/h this aerodynamically shaped Ford 3L GT designed by Len Baily was built as a result of the displacement limit rule change of 1967 by the FIA. First appeared at Brands Hatch, Kent 1968.

Available Now

MINI Cooper S
Code: **A55310**

One of the most recognisable vehicles on today's roads the MINI stands out from the crowd and has immense popularity all over Europe and beyond. They come in all colours and designs, and this, the Cooper S, is no exception.

Available Now

LARGE STARTER SETS

www.airfix.com

GIFT SETS

Gift Sets all contain paint, adhesive and brushes. The following pages have something for everyone.

A brilliant way to start the fantastic hobby of Airfix modelling!

RE-INTRODUCED
One Step for Man...

One Step for Man... 50th Anniversary of Apollo 11 Moon Landing

Code: **A50106**

50 years ago, American Neil Armstrong became the first man to walk on the Moon. The astronaut stepped onto the Moon's surface, in the Sea of Tranquility, at 02:56 GMT, nearly 20 minutes after first opening the hatch on the Eagle landing craft. Armstrong had earlier reported the lunar module's safe landing at 20:17 GMT with the words: 'Houston, Tranquility Base here. The Eagle has landed.' As he put his left foot down first Armstrong declared: 'That's one small step for man, one giant leap for mankind.' He described the surface as being like powdered charcoal and the landing craft only left a small indentation on the surface.

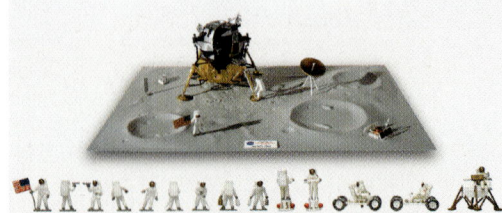

Available May-19

Please visit **www.airfix.com/catalogue2019** to locate your nearest Airfix stockist

RAF Centenary: 1918 – 2018
Sopwith Camel 2F.1
Supermarine Spitfire Mk.Ia
Eurofighter Typhoon F.Mk.2

On 1st April 1918, the amalgamation of the Royal Naval Air Service and the Royal Flying Corps into a single air fighting force saw the birth of the Royal Air Force and with it, the establishment of the world's first independent air arm. Over the course of its illustrious history, perhaps no other aircraft type has represented the strength and capability of a modern RAF more effectively than the fighter, defending Britain from attack, whilst also captivating the imagination of the general public.

Flown by heroes and carrying the pride of a grateful nation into the air with them, these aircraft are often regarded as the most exciting machines created by man and during the past 100 years, the Royal Air Force has been equipped with some of the most capable fighting aeroplanes the world has ever seen.

Available Now — Code: **A50181**

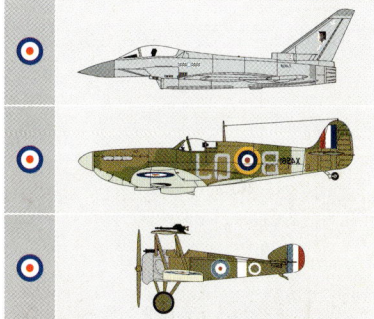

Supermarine Spitfire Mk.Vb
Messerschmitt Bf109E Dogfight Double

Code: **A50160**

Between June 1940 and November 1942 the small but strategically important island of Malta, situated in the Mediterranean Sea, became the most heavily bombed place on earth when first Italian and then German bombers attempted to force the island to surrender. At the height of the battle, cannon armed and tropicalized Spitfire Mk.Vbs were used against Messerschmitt Bf109Es.

Available Now

Avro Vulcan B Mk2 XH558

Code: **A50097**

XH558 was the last Vulcan to leave RAF service, flying on from 1986 to 1993 as the single RAF Display Vulcan. Her final flight was on 23rd March 1993 to Bruntingthorpe. In 1997, a small team headed by Dr Robert Pleming started to put together a plan to return her to flight. After 14 years Vulcan XH558 roared into the air again.

Available Now

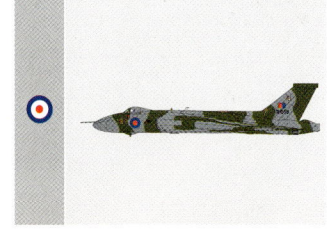

www.airfix.com

GIFT SETS

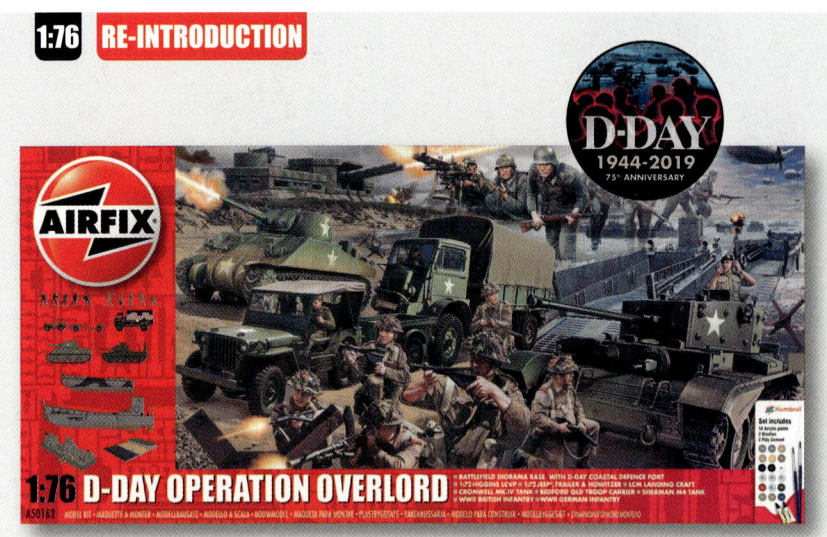

D-Day Operation Overlord

Early on the morning of June 6th 1944 the combined forces of the Allied armies landed on the Normandy beaches in Northern France in the most ambitious and important operation of the Second World War. This collection comes from the Normandy beach-head, with tanks, landing craft, trucks, a gun emplacement, soldiers and a diorama base to enable you to recreate this momentous day.

Available April-19

Code: **A50162A**

D-Day Battlefront

Depicting a scene that is typical of the many meetings of opposing forces in the battles of Northern Europe in 1944, this set contains a Sherman and Tiger Tank, British Paratroops and German Infantry, a Forward Command Post and base to set everything on to.

Available April-19

Code: **A50009A**

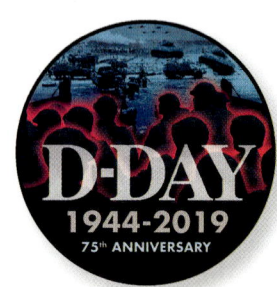

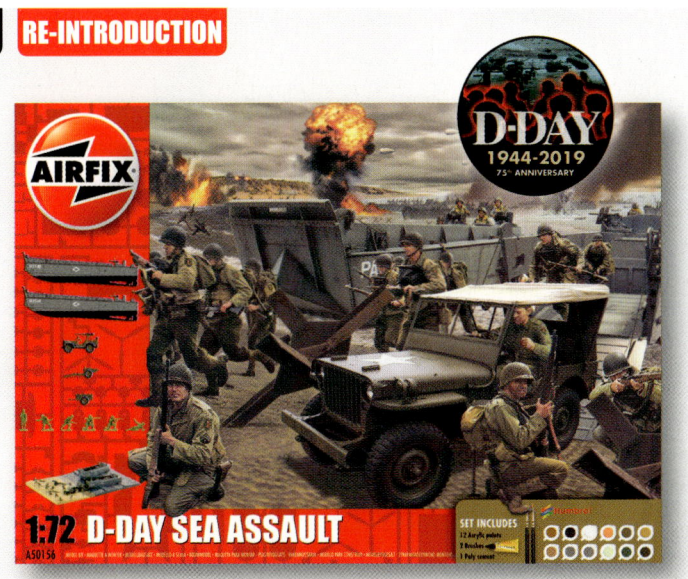

75th Anniversary D-Day Sea Assault Set

Thousands of Allied troops landed on the beaches of Normandy, France in June 1944. This set allows for a diorama of the beach landings to be created with the two landing craft, soldier figures, bespoke base and Jeep.

Available April-19 Code: **A50156A**

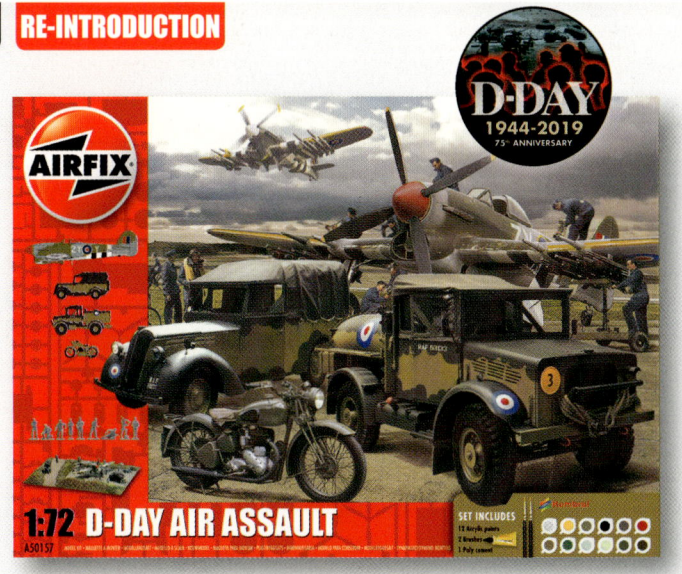

75th Anniversay D-Day Air Assault Set

Aircraft played a crucial role in the invasion, and the Hawker Typhoon was used across the battlefield keeping enemy tanks and troops away from the advancing front line. Set includes a Tilly and Bedford Refuelling truck along with a set of R.A.F Personell.

Available April-19 Code: **A50157A**

GIFT SETS

www.airfix.com

RMS Titanic RE-INTRODUCTION

R.M.S. Titanic Gift Set

Code: **A50146A**

The RMS Titanic will go down in maritime history as not just the largest and most luxurious passenger ship afloat upon its launch in 1912, but also as the most infamous, due to its now legendary maiden voyage. Despite warnings given to it by other ships, the Titanic steamed into the side of an iceberg on the night of the 14th April 1912. This tore a large hole in the side of the hull, overwhelming the ship's famed, watertight compartments. As water poured in, the order was given to abandon ship, with women and children being prioritised over the men. Of the 2224 passengers on board, just 711 survived, with the vast majority being women and children of the first and second class. Today, 100 years after its maiden voyage and sinking, the legend of the Titanic continues to capture the imagination of the world.

Available June-19

Please visit www.airfix.com/catalogue2019 to locate your nearest Airfix stockist

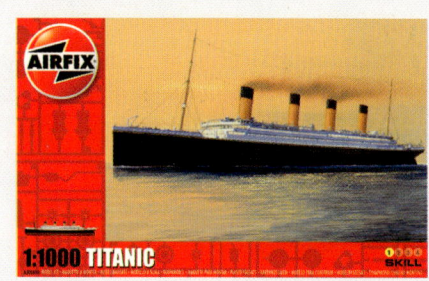

1:1000 NEW

R.M.S. Titanic Starter Set

The legend of the Titanic continues to capture the imagination of the world. Added to this year's range is a smaller scale model available as a Starter Set. Ideal for beginners or those with less display space, this set comes complete with six paints, glue and two paintbrushes. A fantastic addition to your collection or a welcome gift for any time of the year.

Available June-19 Code: A55314

1:700 RE-INTRODUCTION

R.M.S. Titanic Gift Set

Code: A50164A

Built by Harland and Wolff in Belfast, Northern Ireland, and launched on May 31st 1911, the Royal Mail Steam Ship Titanic was one of three Olympic-class passenger ships built for the White Star line. The largest, most luxuriant passenger ship ever built at the time, Titanic sailed on her maiden voyage from Southampton to New York on 10 April 1912. Captained by Edward J Smith, Titanic left Southampton setting course across the Atlantic for New York with over 2,000 people on board. The passengers ranged from the poorest emigrants traveling steerage (third class) to the rich and famous such as John Jacob Astor and his wife Madeleine Force Astor, millionariess Margaret "Molly" Brown, the White Star Line's managing director J. Bruce Ismay and the ship's builder Thomas Andrews.

This model of the famous and tragically doomed Titanic comes in pre-coloured plastic making it suitable for both beginners as well as advanced modellers of all ages.

Available June-19

GIFT SETS

www.airfix.com

MILITARY AIRCRAFT

Although the history of aviation is much more than war machines, the development of aviation was unquestionably stimulated by conflict. The aeroplane became the most important military weapon during the horrors of the Great War and as these early airmen struggled to gain air superiority, the celebrity of the fighter pilot was born. The exploits of military airmen and their enigmatic aeroplanes continue to captivate millions of enthusiasts to this day.

1:72 / 1:48 / 1:24 SCALE MILITARY AIRCRAFT

38

Please visit www.airfix.com/catalogue2019 to locate your nearest Airfix stockist

1:72 / 1:48 / 1:24 SCALE MILITARY AIRCRAFT

www.airfix.com

1:72 SCALE

This smaller scale is perfect for those models where you want a more simple and faster construction.

There are even more exiting additions this year!

Focke-Wulf Fw190A-8

First flying in 1939, the Focke-Wulf Fw190 proved to be an immediate threat to RAF fighters when introduced in late 1941, being faster and more manoeuvrable than the Spitfire V then in service. This A8 version was the most numerous and heavily armed variant and entered service in 1944 as an attempt to stop Allied daylight raids, however, by then new Allied fighters had begun to out-class it.

Available Feb-19 Code: **A01020A**

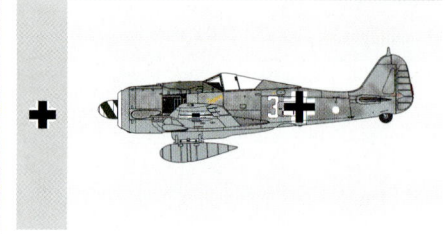

Curtiss Hawk 81-A-2

Flying the P-40B, the Flying Tigers, known officially as the 1st American Volunteer Group, were a unit of the Republic of China Air Force. At one time this aircraft was part of the Fighter Collection at IWM Duxford for more information please visit www.fighter-collection.com

Available June-19 Code: **A01003**

Please visit www.airfix.com/catalogue2019 to locate your nearest Airfix stockist

North American P-51D Mustang™

Code: **A01004A**

Without question, the North American P-51D Mustang was one of the finest fighter aircraft of the Second World War and helped to secure air superiority for the Allies over occupied Europe. Able to escort USAAF bombers all the way to their targets deep into Germany, Mustang pilots would pounce on any Luftwaffe fighters sent to challenge them.

Available Now

Mitsubishi A6M2b Zero

Code: **A01005**

The A6M2b Zero fighter marked the beginning of a new era in naval aviation and was the first shipboard fighter capable of outperforming land-based aircraft. With its tight turning radius, it was an extremely deadly weapon in a dogfight.

Available Now

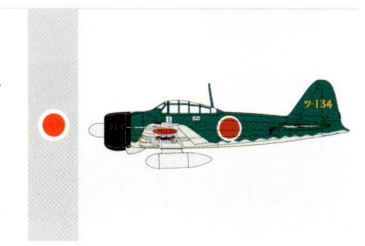

Messerschmitt Bf109E-4

Code: **A01008A**

When the diminutive Messerschmitt Bf109 entered service in February 1935, it was one of the most advanced aircraft in the world, clearly heralding the future of fighter design. Produced in greater quantities than any other fighter aircraft, the Bf109 served throughout WWII and was flown by many of the world's most successful air aces.

Available Now

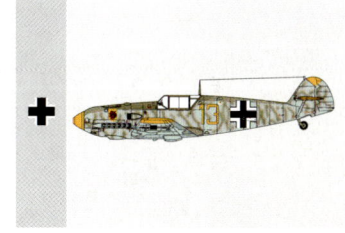

Hawker Hurricane Mk.I

Code: **A01010**

The original fabric-covered winged Hurricane Mk I was upgraded with a de Havilland or Rotol constant speed metal propeller, metal-covered wings, armour and other improvements. In 1939, the RAF had taken on about 500 of this later design.

Available Now

Supermarine Spitfire Mk.I

Code: **A01071B**

The first production Spitfire Mk.I was delivered to RAF No.19 Squadron at Duxford on 4th August 1938 and heralded the arrival of a future aviation icon. With various upgraded marks of this classic fighter serving throughout WWII, the Spitfire is arguably the most famous fighter aircraft to ever take to the skies.

Available Now

Fokker E.III Eindecker

Code: **A01087**

The E.III variant of this historically important fighter aircraft began to arrive on the Western Front at the end of 1915 and proved to be the definitive version of the aircraft. Produced in larger numbers than any other Eindecker, the arrival of large numbers of E.IIIs allowed the Luftstreitkrafte to deploy specialist fighter 'hunting' squadrons for the first time.

Available Now

1:72 SCALE MILITARY AIRCRAFT

Hawker Typhoon Mk.IB

Designed initially to replace the Hawker Hurricane as the complimentary high-altitude fighter to the Supermarine Spitfire, the Typhoon instead found its fame as a low altitude ground attack aircraft, spearheading the airborne assault through occupied Europe after D-Day. Designed around the enormous 24 cylinder Napier Sabre engine, the Typhoon had a tough gestation before maturing as a capable, low level fighter bomber, devastating German armour in Normandy and beyond.

Available Feb-19 — Code: **A02041A**

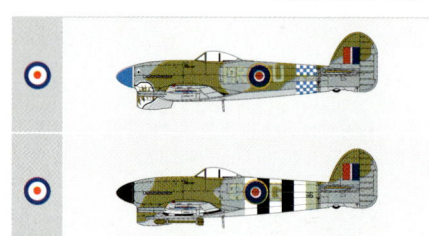

Gloster Gladiator Mk.I/Mk.II

The last of the RAF's biplane fighters, the Gladiator had some modern features, such as an enclosed cockpit, as well as an armament of four machine guns. Still in service at the outbreak of the war, the Gladiator proved to be a capable biplane fighter, but was outclassed against modern monoplane opposition. The mount of some of the RAF's most famous pilots, such as Pat Pattle and Roald Dahl, preserved Gladiators can still be seen flying today at Duxford and Old Warden air displays.

Available June-19 — Code: **A02052A**

de Havilland Vampire T.11 / J-28C

First entering RAF service in 1952, the De Havilland Vampire T.11 trainer was the final UK variant of Britain's second operational jet fighter and the first advanced jet trainer to adopt a side-by-side seating configuration. Unusually, the forward section of the fuselage was constructed of plywood, adopting manufacturing techniques perfected on the famous wartime Mosquito.

Available Now — Code: **A02058A**

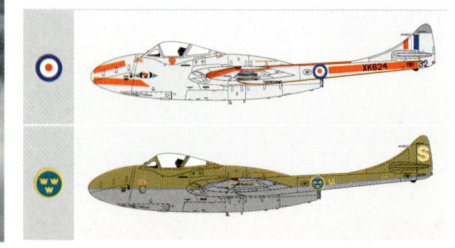

Please visit www.airfix.com/catalogue2019 to locate your nearest Airfix stockist

Hunting Percival Jet Provost T.4

The Jet Provost was introduced in the late 1950s and quickly became the RAF's premier basic jet trainer. The T3 model, introduced in 1959, featured an uprated engine and an improved canopy design, offering the side by side seated pilot and pupil a much improved view. Its reliability and strength also added to its suitability as a jet trainer and the addition of wing tip tanks on the T3 also added to its endurance. The T4 model was visually identical to the T3, but featured a more powerful engine and both variants served with a wide variety of RAF squadrons and training colleges.

Available Feb-19 Code: **A02107**

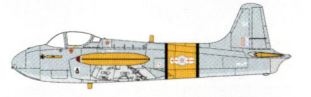

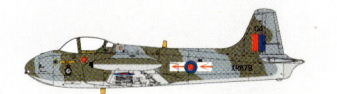

Messerschmitt Bf109G-6

Code: **A02029A**

The "G" version of the Luftwaffe's formidable fighter had an engine with increased power to improve its performance. This was required due to the new aircraft the Allies were introducing on all fronts.

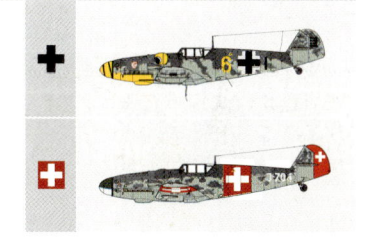

Available Now

Boulton Paul Defiant Mk.I

Code: **A02069**

Often maligned as a failure, the Boulton Paul Defiant proved its effectiveness as a night fighter during the Blitz by shooting down more enemy aircraft than any other type. Built as a "turret fighter" and often mistaken for Hurricanes by the Luftwaffe the Defiant pilots proved themselves during the Battle of Britain.

Available Now

Grumman F4F-4 Wildcat™

Code: **A02070**

The Grumman F4F-4 Wildcat was an American carrier-based fighter aircraft that began service with both the United States Navy and the British Royal Navy with high air combat kill-to-loss ratios. The Wildcat was built throughout the war to serve on escort carriers where larger and heavier fighters could not be used.

Available Now

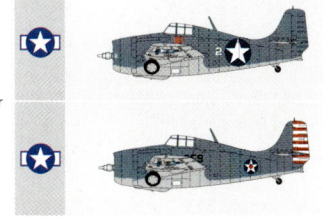

Grumman Martlet Mk.IV™

Code: **A02074**

At a time when the Royal Navy were desperately in need of an effective single engine fighter, the new American F4F Wildcat was seen as the ideal solution and was immediately pressed into service. Known as the Martlet in Fleet Air Arm service, this diminutive aircraft was used operationally right through to the end of the war in Europe.

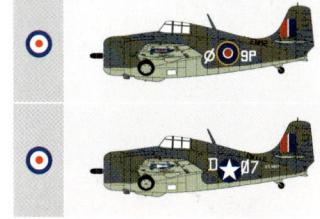

Available Now

1:72 SCALE MILITARY AIRCRAFT

www.airfix.com

1:72 SCALE MILITARY AIRCRAFT

Royal Aircraft Factory BE2c
Code: **A02101**

The stable flight characteristics of the government designed Royal Aircraft Factory BE2c made it an ideal choice for use as a home defence night fighter aircraft. It famously claimed the destruction of the first German Airship over Britain on 3rd September 1916, earning pilot Lt. William Leefe Robinson a Victoria Cross.

Available Now

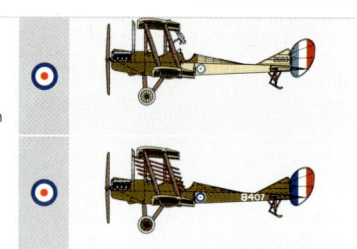

Supermarine Spitfire Mk.VA
Code: **A02102**

Without doubt, the Supermarine Spitfire was one of the most important aircraft of WWII, with more being produced that any other British aircraft type – it was also in production throughout the war. The Mk.V version of the Spitfire was produced in greater numbers than any other mark and gave the RAF a combat advantage throughout most of 1941.

Available Now

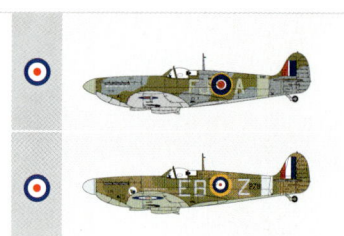

Hunting Percival Jet Provost T.3
Code: **A02103**

For most RAF pilots serving between 1960 and 1988, the Hunting Aircraft (BAC) Jet Provost will be an extremely familiar aircraft to them. Forming the backbone of RAF pilot training during this period, the Jet Provost was distinctive by its broad fuselage profile, which allowed for a relatively spacious side-by-side cockpit arrangement.

Available Now

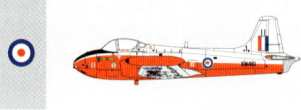

Royal Aircraft Factory BE2c
Code: **A02104**

Designed specifically to allow aircrews to effectively secure vital reconnaissance imagery from above the battlefields of the Western Front, the Royal Aircraft Factory BE2c Scout was an aircraft with very few vices. Easy to fly and extremely stable in the air, the aircraft allowed Allied military planners to obtain clear and detailed photographs of enemy positions.

Available Now

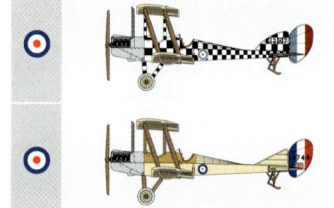

Folland Gnat T.1
Code: **A02105**

The diminutive Folland Gnat was originally developed as a light and affordable jet fighter, but went on to be used extensively by the Royal Air Force as an advanced fast jet training aircraft. Entering RAF service in 1959, the Gnat was responsible for training many hundreds of future fast jet pilots during its 20 year service career.

Available Now

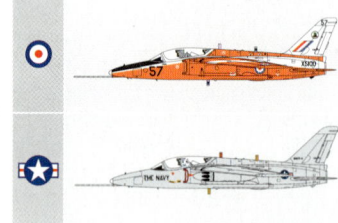

de Havilland Tiger Moth
Code: **A02106**

A familiar sight at airfields all over the world, the de Havilland Tiger Moth primary trainer made its first flight back in 1931 and went on to provide British and Commonwealth air forces with thousands of trained pilots for their operational squadrons. Performing a similar role to this day, the Tiger Moth allows prospective Warbird pilots to gain experience in flying a tail-dragger aircraft.

Available Now

Please visit www.airfix.com/catalogue2019 to locate your nearest Airfix stockist

1:72 NEW SCHEMES RE-INTRODUCTION

Douglas™ A-4B/Q Skyhawk™

Code: **A03029A**

The A-4B was the second variant of the Skyhawk and one of the first to see combat in the skies over Vietnam, where it was involved in the early stages of the conflict, with later versions serving throughout the campaign. Due to its small size, the A4 was able to operate off the smaller World War Two era, Essex Class carriers, but could still carry a useful payload to its target.

Available Feb-19

Messerschmitt Bf110C

Code: **A03080A**

Championed by Hermann Goering, the Messerschmitt Bf 110 Destroyer, (or Heavy Fighter) concept was certainly sound in theory, giving these slightly larger aircraft much greater range and devastating firepower. Unfortunately, the increase in size and weight left the Destroyers vulnerable to the more manoeuvrable single engined fighters of the RAF.

Available Now

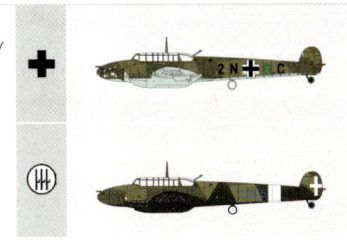

BAe Hawk T.Mk.1A

Code: **A03085A**

The agile and reliable BAe Hawk T.1 has been providing the Royal Air Force with an effective advanced jet pilot training platform for over 40 years, replacing the Folland Gnat in this role. With over 1000 aircraft produced, the Hawk has also proved to be one of Britain's most lucrative post war aviation export successes.

Available Now

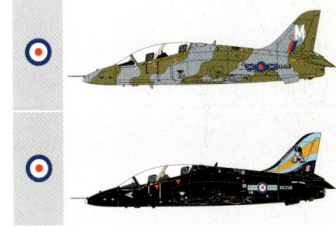

Junkers Ju87B-1 Stuka

Code: **A03087**

The Junkers JU87 or Stuka, was a two-man ground attack aircraft and dive bomber which first took to the skies in 1935. The Stuka is famous for delivering the single most deadly assault on British territory in history on the afternoon of 4th July 1940 when thirty three of them sank the 5,500 ton anti-aircraft ship HMS Foylebank in Portland Harbour.

Available Now

Messerschmitt Me262A-1a

Code: **A03088**

Described by famous British test pilot Eric 'Winkle' Brown as the most formidable aircraft of WWII, the Messerschmitt Me 262 was a quantum leap in aviation performance and stands as one of the most significant aircraft in the history of flight. Had the Luftwaffe deployed large numbers of these impressive fighters, they would have taken a heavy toll of Allied aircraft.

Available Now

1:72 SCALE MILITARY AIRCRAFT

www.airfix.com

NEW PARTS Messerschmitt Me262A-2a 'Sturmvogel'

1:72 SCALE MILITARY AIRCRAFT

1:72 | NEW PARTS | NEW SCHEMES

Messerschmitt Me262A-2a 'Sturmvogel'

Despite being the most advanced aircraft of WWII, Adolf Hitler insisted that the Me262 be developed into a fast attack bomber, diverting valuable resources from much needed fighter production. Known as the 'Stormbird' the attack version included hard points for two 500kg bombs under the nose of the aircraft, with its speed making it almost invulnerable from Allied air interception.

Available-Oct-19 | Code: **A03090**

Please visit www.airfix.com/catalogue2019 to locate your nearest Airfix stockist

1:72 RE-INTRODUCTION

Bristol Blenheim Mk.I

Code: **A04016**

The Britol Blenheim bomber was ordered "off the drawing board", and first deliveries to No 114 Sqn began in 1937. By the time of the Munich crisis in September 1938 sixteen home-based bomber squadrons were equipped with the type.

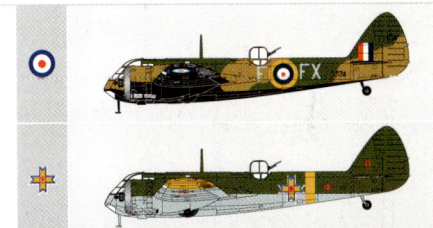

Available June-19

Messerschmitt Me262B-1a/U1

Code: **A04062**

As the first operational jet fighter in the world, initial Messerschmitt Me262s combat operations were flown by single seat aircraft, piloted by some of the Luftwaffe's most experienced airmen. A two seat trainer version soon followed, which allowed new pilots to acquaint themselves with this advanced technology, without their conversion from piston power being their first solo jet flight.

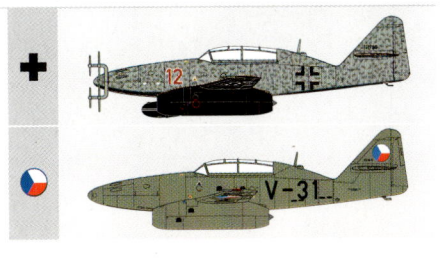

Available Now

www.airfix.com

1:72 SCALE MILITARY AIRCRAFT

NEW MOULD
Mikoyan-Gurevich MiG-17F 'Fresco'

The end of the Second World War saw the victorious Allied nations desperately attempting to secure details of German jet technology and high speed research data, information which could be applied to their own jet projects. Using this information and engine technology obtained from Britain, the Soviet Union introduced the diminutive Mikoyan-Gurevich MiG-15 in 1949 one of the most capable of the early jet fighters and even as this aircraft was proving effective during the Korean War, the Soviets were already working on its successor. The larger and faster MiG-17 Fresco may have given the appearance of being nothing more than a larger incarnation of its predecessor, however, this was in fact a completely redesigned aircraft, incorporating many improvements over the MiG-15 and a significant upgrade in Soviet jet capability.

Please visit www.airfix.com/catalogue2019 to locate your nearest Airfix stockist

Mikoyan-Gurevich MiG-17F 'Fresco'

1:72 **NEW MOULD**

The MiG-17 was designed to perform the role of bomber killer and was never intended as a dogfighter, however its exceptional agility would allow this aircraft to score combat victories over much heavier and more modern American designs. Dismissing the aircraft as nothing more than an upgraded MiG-15, the Vietnam War proved to be something of a sobering experience for the US Air Force, as some of their most modern aircraft would fall victim to the guns of the MiG-17, even though this had itself been superseded by more modern designs. Lighter and much more manoeuvrable than the US aircraft, the subsonic MiG-17 would claim victories over such aircraft as the F-105 Thunderchief and McDonnell Douglas Phantom, which would result in the US developing new agile air superiority fighters, in the years immediately following the end of the conflict.

Possessing both excellent performance and being easy to maintain, the rugged MiG-17 was produced in large numbers and became the standard Warsaw Pact fighter from the mid 1950s and for the next decade, with aircraft produced under licence in both China and Poland. An extremely cost effective aircraft, it was an attractive fighter option for many of the world's smaller air forces and more than thirty overseas nations would eventually operate the type. Perversely, for a nation against which the MiG-17 was designed to combat, America would become home to significant numbers of these aircraft, most coming into the hands of private collectors, but a small number used in dissimilar aircraft trials and to perfect combat techniques against smaller, more agile jet fighters. Two beautifully restored examples have also been popular display performers on the US Airshow circuit over the years.

Available Nov-19   Code: **A03091**

www.airfix.com

1:72 SCALE MILITARY AIRCRAFT

Supermarine Swift FR.5
Code: **A04003**

The Swift still holds the honour of being the first swept-wing jet fighter into RAF service. The FR.5 proved itself in the reconnaissance role, in 1957 and 1959 Swifts won the NATO 'Royal Flush' reconnaissance competition, conclusively beating off the best types other nations could offer.

Available Now

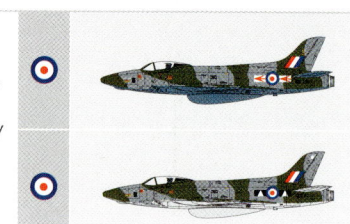

Bristol Beaufighter TF.X
Code: **A04019**

The Bristol Beaufighter "Beau" was a British long-range heavy fighter which had a long career serving in almost all theatres of war during WW2 as night fighter and then as a fighter bomber.

Available Now

Fairey Swordfish Mk.I
Code: **A04053A**

Despite being considered obsolete at the start of the war, the Swordfish served with distinction throughout WWII and outlasted aircraft which were intended as its replacement.

Available Now

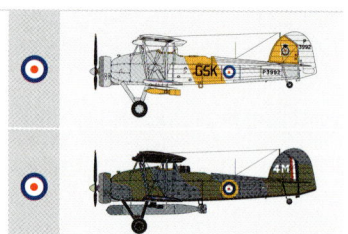

Westland Sea King HC.4
Code: **A04056**

Operated by the Royal Navy, one of the most extensively modified versions of the Westland Sea King is the Westland Commando HC4. First flying on 26 September 1979, this high capacity, iconic aircraft was used extensively for British operations in both Gulf Wars, Falklands War and Afghanistan.

Available Now

Nakajima B5N2 'Kate'
Code: **A04058**

With a much more powerful engine than that of the B5N1, the B5N2 had several other modifications to streamline it. This aircraft is particularly known for its involvement in the attack on Pearl Harbour and the sinking of the United States Navy aircraft carriers Lexington and Hornet.

Available Now

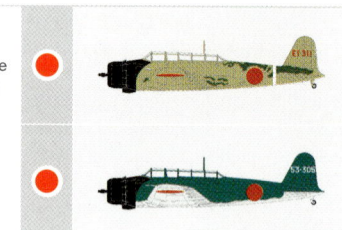

Bristol Blenheim Mk.If
Code: **A04059**

The Bristol Blenheim was conceived as a privately funded high-speed civilian aircraft, intended to wrestle the record for the fastest civilian aircraft in Europe away from the Germans. Successfully achieving this, it immediately attracted the attention of the RAF – at the outbreak of WWII, the Blenheim was available in more numbers than any other RAF aircraft.

Available Now

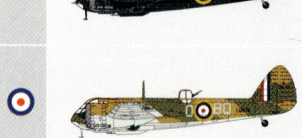

Please visit www.airfix.com/catalogue2019 to locate your nearest Airfix stockist

WWII RAF Bomber Re-supply Set

As the air war over occupied Europe progressed and developed, so did the equipment used by the RAF and its Bomber Command. Specialist vehicles were introduced to supply arms and equipment to waiting machines and maintenance tasks were made easier through the introduction of specialist equipment.

Available Now — Code: **A05330**

WWII USAAF Bomber Re-supply Set

As US bomber operations began to take place at airfields all over Southern England from the summer of 1942, the vehicles used in servicing Liberators and Flying Fortresses were slowly changing from the standard RAF support vehicles, to specialised US Air Force equipment. From fuel trailers to bomb trolleys, Bedfords were quickly being replaced by Chevrolets. The Autocar U-7144-T 4X4 tractor unit was used extensively by the US military from 1942 onwards and was certainly found on most, if not all USAAF airfields in Britain, particularly in conjunction with the standard F-1 fuel trailer. With many aircraft requiring refuelling on a daily basis, it was usual for each base to have numerous examples of the U-7144-T available at any one time.

The Chevrolet M6 bomb utility 4X4 service truck was capable of carrying a small number of bombs in its own right, but was more commonly used in conjunction with the M5 bomb trailer. Indeed, it was capable of towing up to five fully loaded M5s.

Available Now — Code: **A06304**

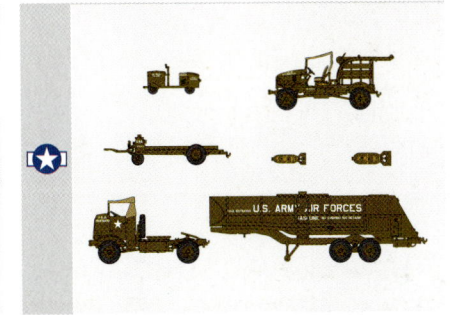

Eighth Air Force: Boeing B-17G™ & Bomber Re-Supply Set

Code: **A12010**

The United States Army Air Force (USAAF) Eighth Air Force was created during World War II to support the Allied invasion of German occupied Europe by flying day-time strategic bombing missions from bases in Eastern England.

Available Now

www.airfix.com

1:72 SCALE MILITARY AIRCRAFT

Nakajima B5N1 'Kate'
Code: **A04060**

The Nakajima B5N1 'Kate' was the most numerous Japanese torpedo bomber of the Second World War and while primarily operated as a torpedo bomber from carriers, it also saw service as a land based bomber..

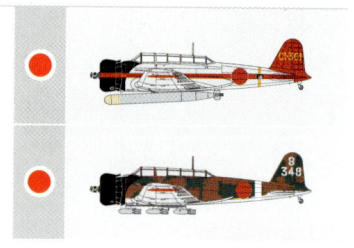

Available Now

Westland Sea King HAR.3/Mk.43
Code: **A04063**

The Westland Sea King HAS.3 served in the Search and Rescue role for almost 38 years, saving countless lives and earning the admiration of a grateful British public. Possessing impressive endurance and all-weather flying capability, the stable and reliable Sea King allowed crews to carry out rescue missions in the most challenging flying conditions imaginable.

Available Now

English Electric Lightning F.6

As the only all-British built Mach 2 plus capable fighter aircraft, the English Electric Lightning occupies a unique place in aviation history and remains one of the finest achievements of the British aviation industry. Possessing incredible performance, this Cold War warrior entered service in 1960 and became Britain's primary interceptor for the following two decades.

Available Now Code: **A05042A**

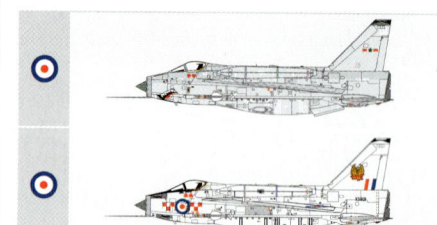

Bristol Beaufighter TF.10
Code: **A05043**

Originally entering RAF service as a heavy fighter/night fighter in August 1940, the Bristol Beaufighter proved to be an extremely versatile aircraft. Perhaps best known as a Coastal Command strike aircraft, Beaufighters were capable of launching savage attacks against all manner of Axis shipping targets.

Available Now

North American B25C/D Mitchell™
Code: **A06015**

The B-25 Mitchell, a twin-engine medium bomber developed just before the Second World War, was synonymous with the Doolittle Raid, the attack on Tokyo by USAAF Mitchells. The B-25 featured a 'gull' wing and a whole host of armaments. Early versions had glazed noses, but as the type matured, more and more guns were added to the nose of the aircraft.

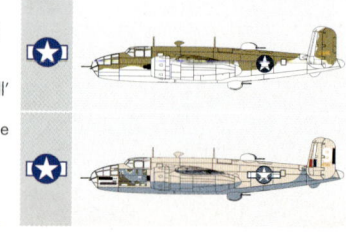

Available Now

Please visit www.airfix.com/catalogue2019 to locate your nearest Airfix stockist

1:72 NEW SCHEMES

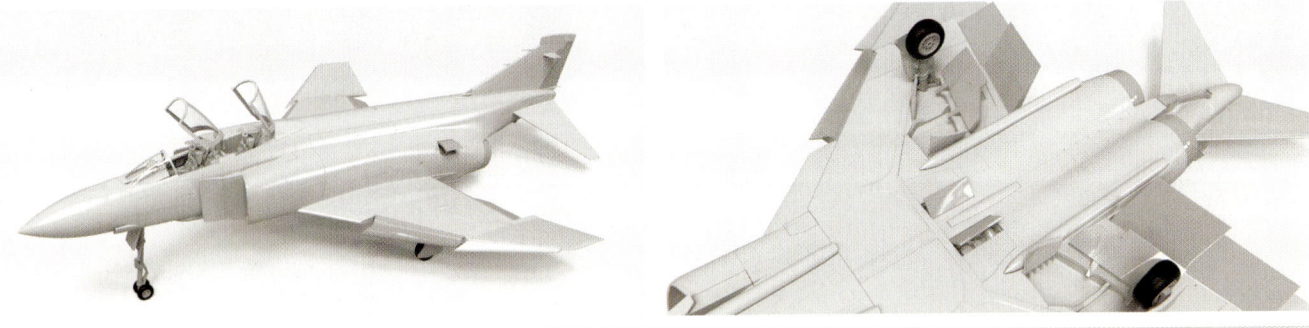

McDonnell Douglas Phantom™ FG.1 RAF

Available Sept-19 — Code: **A06019**

With the RAF already operating Phantoms initially intended for the Royal Navy at Leuchars air base in Fife, the withdrawal of HMS Ark Royal in 1978 meant that they also inherited the rest of the Fleet Air Arm Phantom fleet. Nos 43 and 111 Squadrons would use the Phantom FG.1 to defend Britain's airspace until 1989, when they both converted to the BAe Tornado F.3.

1:72 NEW PARTS NEW SCHEMES

McDonnell Douglas Phantom™ FGR.2

As the Royal Air Force were looking to update their strike and close air support capabilities in the 1950s and 60s, they were initially expecting indigenous British designs to fulfil both of these roles, but spiralling development costs and government intervention saw them forced to look overseas for their new aircraft. As one of the world's most successful multi-role jet aircraft, the McDonnell Douglas Phantom was selected for both the Royal Navy and the RAF and even though it was procured at a time of great uncertainty for the British aviation industry, it proved to be both a capable and popular aircraft in UK service.

Available Feb-19 — Code: **A06017**

1:72

McDonnell Douglas Phantom™ FG.1

Code: **A06016**

The Royal Navy Phantoms operated from the carrier HMS Ark Royal and were the only Phantoms operated at sea outside the USA. But after the retirement of the Navy's large aircraft carriers the Phantoms were passed to the RAF. In both air arms the Spey powered Phantoms proved to be a popular machine, able to carry large loads of ordinance a long way.

Available Now

1:72 SCALE MILITARY AIRCRAFT

www.airfix.com

NEW MOULD
Blackburn Buccaneer S Mk.2 RN

1:72 SCALE MILITARY AIRCRAFT

The mighty Blackburn Buccaneer was one of the most capable low-level strike aircraft of the Cold War period, originally entering Royal Navy service in 1962 to counter the significant threat of a massive Soviet Naval expansion programme. Rather than face the crippling cost of building new ships of their own to meet this threat, British thinking at the time was to use their new strike jet to destroy the Soviet ships with a combination of conventional and nuclear weapons. Capable of extremely high speeds at low level, the Buccaneer proved to be the ideal aircraft to keep the Warsaw Pact countries on their toes, even though the performance of the first Buccaneers to enter service was affected by a lack of power from their two de Havilland Gyron Junior engines.

Blackburn Buccaneer S Mk.2 RN

1:72 NEW MOULD

Available Sept-19 Code: **A06021**

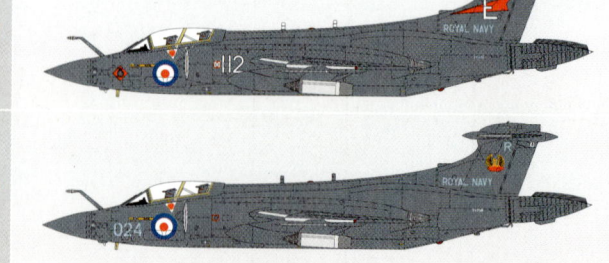

Please visit www.airfix.com/catalogue2019 to locate your nearest Airfix stockist

Operating from the decks of Britain's relatively small aircraft carriers, the Buccaneer had to be tough and its rugged, no nonsense design approach was underlined rather effectively by the aircraft's manufacture and flight testing procedure. Constructed at Blackburn Aviation's Brough facility, each assembled Buccaneer was transported by road, pulled behind a truck on its own undercarriage. They would make a journey of around 16 miles down winding country lanes and across bridges with sharp bends to the company's Holme-on-Spalding Moor facility, where they would undergo final checks and flight testing.

Addressing most of the issues which prevented the early aircraft from realizing their full potential, the Buccaneer S.2 was a much improved platform, boasting a modified wing, increased fuel capacity and a pair of powerful Rolls Royce Spey engines. This new variant provided the Fleet Air Arm with a truly exceptional strike aircraft, which excelled in the low level environment in which it was tasked to operate. One particularly useful design feature for an aircraft which operated mainly over water was the type of ejection seat fitted in the Buccaneer – in the event of a ditching, the seat would still fire even if the aircraft was submerging. As the Royal Navy retired their larger carriers in 1978, their much loved Buccaneers were transferred to the care of the Royal Air Force, who were already admirers of the many qualities possessed by this aircraft and grateful for this increase in their inventory. At its peak strength in the early 1970s, the Blackburn Buccaneer equipped no fewer than six Royal Air Force Squadrons.

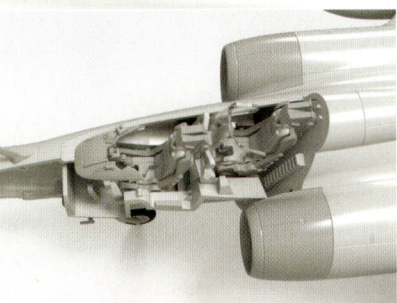

www.airfix.com

1:72 SCALE MILITARY AIRCRAFT

NEW North American B-25B Mitchell 'Doolittle Raid'

North American B-25B Mitchell™
Code: **A06020**

In the aftermath of the Pearl Harbor Raid, America embarked on an audacious plan to strike at the very heart of the Japanese nation and post clear intentions of their resolve for ultimate victory. On 18th April 1942, sixteen B-25B Mitchell bombers lifted off the relatively short deck of USS Hornet and set course for Tokyo – crewed by volunteers, each man would become an American hero.

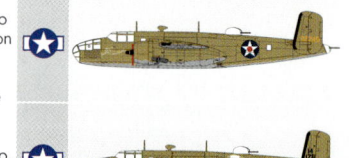

Available Aug-19

Heinkel He.111H-6
Code: **A07007**

Addressing many of the shortcomings of the earlier versions, the Heinkel He.III 'H' series was produced in greater numbers than any other variant. With greater power from the Jumo 211 engines, better defensive armament and heavier weapons loads, these aircraft were used right up until the last days of the war.

Available Now

Avro Lancaster B.III
Code: **A08013A**

During WWII the Avro Lancaster proved to be an exceptional aircraft, possessing a large unobstructed bomb bay, which allowed it to carry some of the largest bombs of the war. At least thirty five Lancasters completed an astonishing 100 missions or more and are referred to by historians and enthusiasts as the 'Lancaster Centurions'.

Available Now

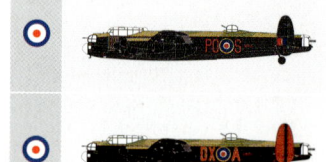

Douglas Dakota Mk.III™
Code: **A08015A**

One of the most important aircraft of the Second World War, the Douglas C-47 Skytrain was the military version of the exceptional DC-3 civilian airliner. Used extensively by the Royal Air Force it was described by General Dwight D Eisenhower as one of the 'Four Tools of Victory' that helped the Allied forces prevail during WWII.

Available Now

Please visit www.airfix.com/catalogue2019 to locate your nearest Airfix stockist

NEW Vickers Wellington Mk.VIII

57

1:72 NEW SCHEMES NEW PARTS

Vickers Wellington Mk.VIII

Code: **A08020**

Britain's most capable bomber at the start of WWII, the Vickers Wellington saw extensive service, including with RAF Coastal Command. Undertaking arduous maritime patrols, Wellington Mk.VIIIs performed reconnaissance, anti-submarine and anti-shipping strike roles in the battle against German U-boats, helping to keep Britain's sea lanes open and preventing Axis forces re-supplying by sea.

Available Aug-19

Vickers Wellington Mk.IA/C

Code: **A08019**

The Wellington was a long range medium bomber designed and developed for the RAF during the 1930s at Vicker's Brooklands factory. Using the fabric-covered geodetic lattice structure originally developed by Barnes Wallis for airships, the airframe quickly gained a reputation for strength and the ability to withstand impressive amounts of enemy fire and punishment when the Wellington went to war in 1939. The Wellington suffered disastrously in unescorted daylight raids at the start of the war but once moved to night operations it was able to operate effectively.

Available Now

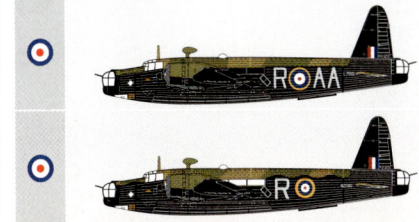

1:72 SCALE MILITARY AIRCRAFT

www.airfix.com

1:72 SCALE MILITARY AIRCRAFT

NEW SCHEMES BOEING B-17G FLYING FORTRESS™

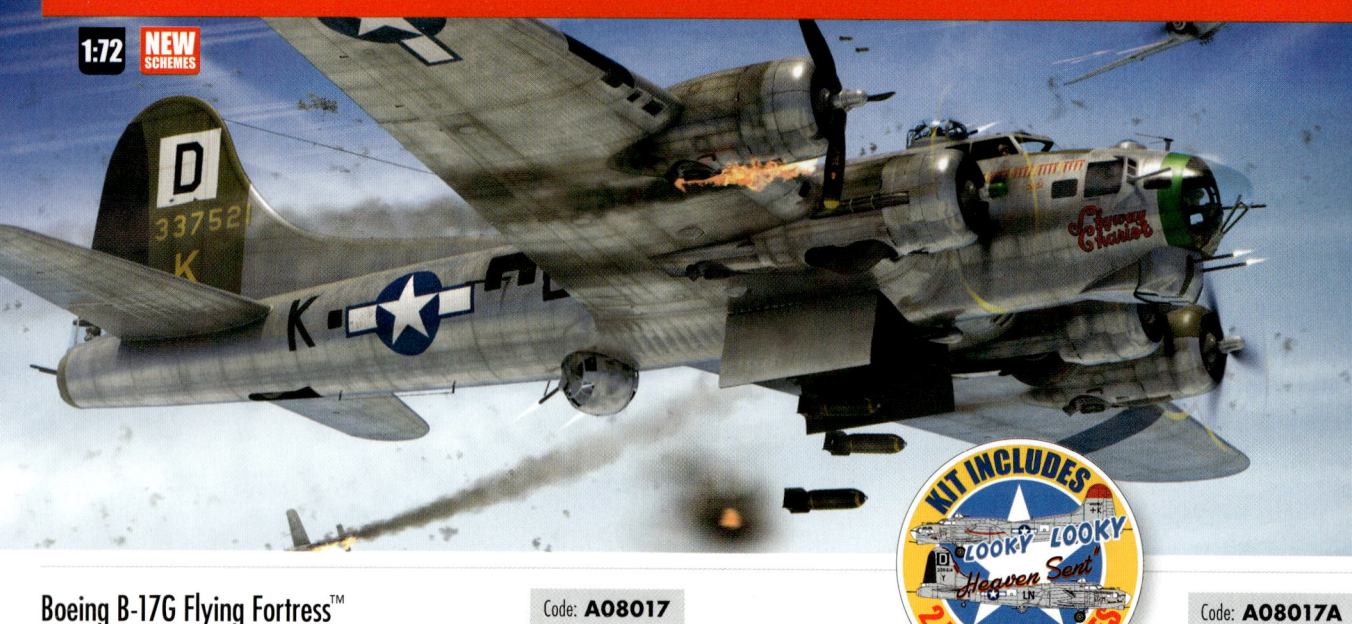

1:72 NEW SCHEMES

KIT INCLUDES 2 EXTRA SCHEMES

Boeing B-17G Flying Fortress™
Code: **A08017**   Code: **A08017A**

The definitive version of this classic USAAF heavy bomber, the Boeing B-17G incorporated a host of improvements on the earlier models of the Flying Fortress. With thirteen machine-guns and optimised defensive firing positions, massed formations of B-17Gs would pound Axis targets on a daily basis, throwing up as much lead at attacking fighters as they possibly could.

Available Now

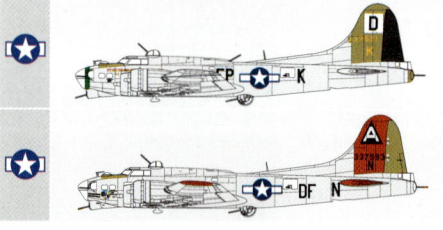

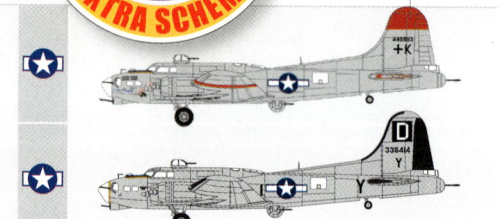

Armstrong Whitworth Whitley Mk.V
Code: **A08016**

The Armstrong Whitworth Whitely saw action right from the first night of WW2 when it dropped leaflets over Germany. It then went on to take part in the first bombing raids over German and Italian territories, making the Whitley an integral part of the RAF's bombing offensive in the war.

Available Now

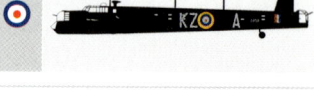

Boeing Fortress Mk.III™
Code: **A08018**

A daylight heavy bomber in USAAF service, the Boeing B-17 (Boeing Fortress Mk.III in RAF service) also had a secretive role. B-17s were flown at night by the RAF's secret 100 Group in the bomber stream and used an electronic warfare system known as 'Airborne Cigar'. This was an attempt to jam German ground controller broadcasts so that the Luftwaffe night fighters could not intercept the bombers.

Available Now

Avro Lancaster B.III (Special) The Dambusters
Code: **A09007**

The Dambusters raid was one the most famous operations of the war. 19 specially modified Lancaster bombers attacked the Mohne, Eder, Sorpe and Ennepe dams, with the Mohne and Eder dams being breached, causing widespread destruction to the German war effort. The dams were breached using the Upkeep mine, or 'bouncing bomb'.

Available Now

Please visit www.airfix.com/catalogue2019 to locate your nearest Airfix stockist

Douglas Dakota Mk.III™ with Willys Jeep®

Code: **A09008**

Having been delivered to the UK in very large numbers, the Dakota Mk III revitalised the RAF's transport. Dakotas served in every theatre of war, most notably in Burma, during the D-Day landings and the airborne assault on Arnhem in 1944.

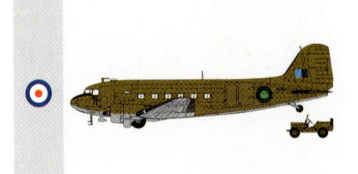

Available Now

Armstrong Whitworth Whitley Mk.VII

Code: **A09009**

The Armstrong Whitworth Whitley was the first 'heavy' bomber to see service with the RAF and proved to be an extremely important aircraft in the early months of WWII. The long-range capabilities of the Whitley proved invaluable to Coastal Command as they could mount extended anti U-boat patrols deep into the Atlantic Ocean.

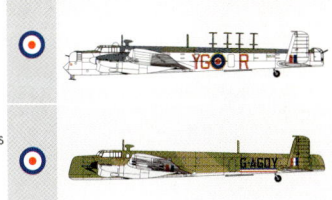

Available Now

Avro Shackleton MR.2

Code: **A11004**

With its four Rolls-Royce Griffon engines giving it the nickname Growler, the Shackleton flew with the RAF from 1949 until 1991! It played a number of roles throughout its service but mainly it was an anti-submarine aircraft and could carry up to 10,000lb of bombs, torpedoes or mines.

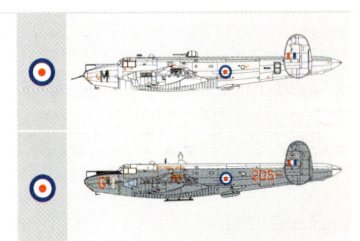

Available Now

Avro Shackleton AEW.2

Code: **A11005**

With the ability to mount patrols for up to twelve hours, the Rolls-Royce Griffon powered Avro Shackleton AEW.2 provided Britain's airborne early warning protection for almost 19 years.

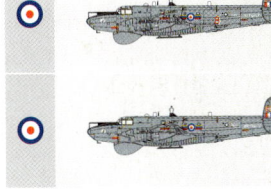

Available Now

Handley Page Victor B.Mk.2 (BS)

Code: **A12008**

Arguably the most capable of Britain's Cold War V-Bombers, the Handley Page Victor is certainly one of the most distinctive jet bombers to ever see service. With its high mounted T-tail and impressive crescent wing, the Victor saw service as a conventional bomber, nuclear bomber and finally as an airborne tanker aircraft, before its eventual retirement in 1993.

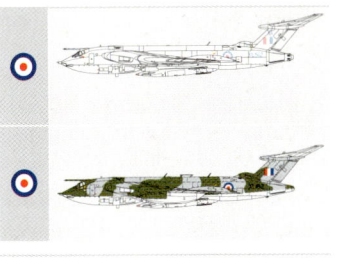

Available Now

Handley Page Victor K.2/SR.2

Code: **A12009**

As the last of Britain's trio of V-bombers to enter service, the Handley Page Victor was arguably the most successful, remaining in RAF service for an impressive 35 years. The final K.2 versions were converted to provide the RAF with an effective air-to-air refuelling aircraft, serving through both the Falklands Conflict and the Gulf War of 1990.

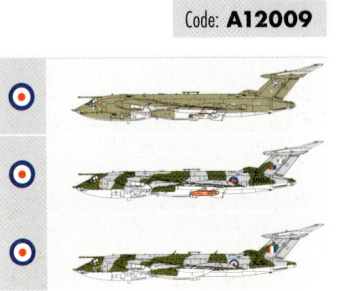

Available Now

1:72 SCALE MILITARY AIRCRAFT

www.airfix.com

1:48 SCALE

This scale is perfect for those models where you want more detail. There are even more exciting additions this year!

NEW MOULD
de Havilland D.H. 82a Tiger Moth

de Havilland D.H.82a Tiger Moth

1:48 NEW MOULD   **Available Dec-19**   **Code: A04104**

The DH.82 Tiger Moth made its first flight in October 1931 and was the result of the Company's founder wanting to produce an aircraft superior to its predecessors, whilst possessing enough appeal to attract interest from several different aviation sectors. Its success resulted in an immediate order from the RAF, who viewed the aircraft as an ideal primary trainer for pilots beginning on their flying careers and destined to fly their latest front line aircraft. Their modest original order was followed up by several subsequent orders and as the world descended into conflict in 1939, the Royal Air Force would have around 500 Tiger Moths. It was a relatively stable and forgiving aircraft to fly, with few handling vices and generally supportive of the odd silly mistake. It has been described as an 'easy aeroplane to fly but a difficult one to fly well', which seemed to have made this the ideal aircraft to serve as a primary/basic trainer for large numbers of future pilots destined for the war effort.

With many Tiger Moths remaining in airworthy condition today, it is interesting to consider that this famous basic training aircraft is still doing the same job as it did during its service introduction in the 1930s. The magnificent Tiger Moth allows potential Warbird pilots the opportunity to gain valuable experience flying a 'taildragger' aircraft, before eventually moving on to display the Spitfires and Mustangs which thrill the crowds at Airshows all over the world.

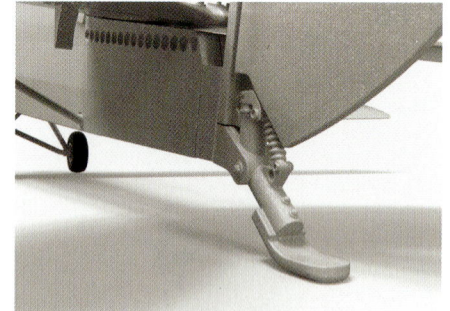

Please visit www.airfix.com/catalogue2019 to locate your nearest Airfix stockist

NEW MOULD Supermarine Spitfire FR Mk.XIV

Supermarine Spitfire FR Mk.XIV

1:48 NEW MOULD

Available Mar-19 **Code: A05135**

The Spitfire Mk.XIV was developed to improve on the high altitude performance of the Spitfire Mk.XII by using the new 65-series twin-stage supercharged Rolls Royce Griffon engine. As the airframe was developed, more and more modifications were made such as the cutback fuselage, bubble canopy and the 'E' wing which featured clipped wingtips and an improved armament. To many this was the ultimate Spitfire. A powerful brute of a machine that could climb at over 5,000ft per minute and achieve a top speed of 446mph (718kph). While operational pilots often found the new machine to be somewhat tricky to handle, once mastered it proved to be a tremendous fighting machine, able to compete on equal terms with almost anything the Luftwaffe had to offer.

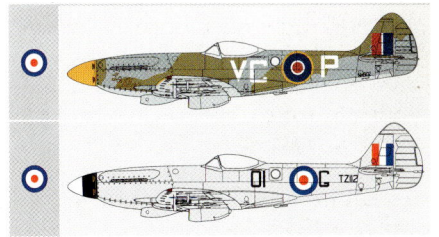

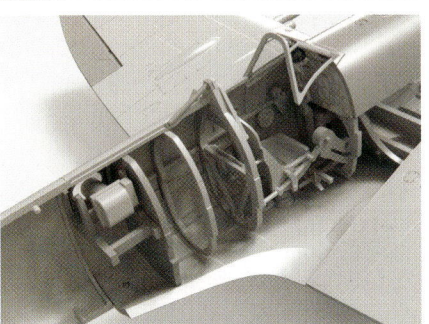

1:48 SCALE MILITARY AIRCRAFT

www.airfix.com

1:48 SCALE MILITARY AIRCRAFT

North American P-51D Mustang™

1:48 NEW PARTS NEW SCHEMES

A thoroughbred fighting aeroplane, the P-51D Mustang was produced in greater numbers than any other variant and introduced a number of improvements over earlier models. With a new wing design, teardrop canopy and lower rear fuselage, the P-51D was the mount of many USAAF aces and became the primary US fighter in the European Theatre, following its introduction in 1944.

Available Nov-19   Code: **A05138**

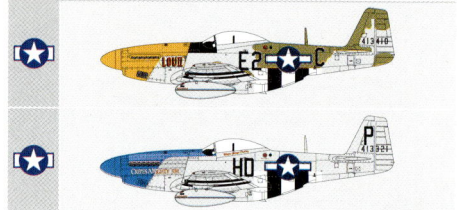

Hawker Hurricane Mk.I Tropical

1:48   Code: **A05129**

The rugged and reliable Hawker Hurricane was arguably the most important fighter aircraft available to the Royal Air Force at the beginning of WWII. Easier to produce and more forgiving to fly than the Spitfire, the Hurricane accounted for more Luftwaffe aircraft destroyed during the Battle of Britain than the rest of Britain's defences combined.

Available Now

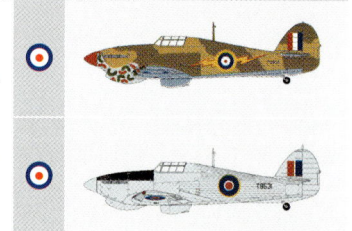

Curtiss P-40B Warhawk

1:48   Code: **A05130**

During the early stages of WWII, the American built Curtiss P-40B proved to be one of the most important fighter aircraft available to Allied Air Forces. Flying with the RAF in North Africa and the American Volunteer Group in China, P-40B was to became one of the most distinctive fighters of the entire war

Available Now

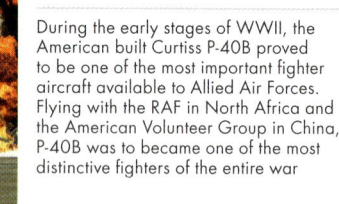

Boulton Paul Defiant NF.1

1:48   Code: **A05132**

Quickly outclassed as a day fighter during the Battle of Britain, the Boulton Paul Defiant would be tasked with protecting Britain from night bombing raids by the Luftwaffe. Not trained to fight at night, Defiant crews would have to develop interception techniques as they fought, but found the aircraft much more suited to this nocturnal fighting environment.

Available Now

North American F-51D Mustang™

1:48   Code: **A05136**

As arguably the finest fighter aircraft of WWII, the Mustang went on to be selected as the USAF primary piston engined fighter after the war, with all other types relegated to secondary roles, or withdrawn from service. The re-designation of USAF aircraft in 1948 saw the P for Pursuit change to F for Fighter, resulting in the Mustang becoming a North American F-51D.

Available Now

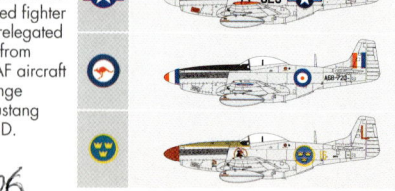

Please visit www.airfix.com/catalogue2019 to locate your nearest Airfix stockist

North American Mustang Mk.IV/P-51K Mustang™

As the North American Mustang was developed as a direct result of a British Air Ministry requirement, it is somehow fitting that the RAF and Commonwealth air forces used the aircraft extensively during WWII. The British designation for the later P-51D version was Mustang IV, with the Dallas built P-51K, which used a different Aeroproducts propeller, referred to as the Mustang IVa.

Available Now — Code: **A05137**

Messerschmitt Bf109E-3/E-4

As the battle hardened Bf109 fighter pilots of the Luftwaffe began operations against Britain following the Dunkirk evacuation, they would be at a disadvantage for the first time. With only enough fuel for limited time over England, any mechanical issue or damage during combat would result in their capture at best, but certainly an end to their war.

Photo: Malcolm V Lowe Collection

Available Now — Code: **A05120B**

Curtiss Tomahawk Mk.II

Code: **A05133**

The first Curtiss Tomahawk fighters to arrive in Britain during WWII operated in the tactical reconnaissance role and were deemed unsuitable for fighter sweeps into German occupied Europe. Later models incorporated a number of improvements and saw extensive service with the Western Desert Air Force.

Available Now

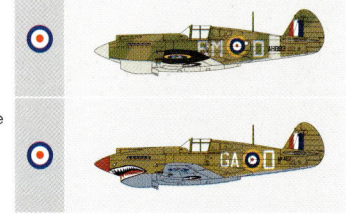

Hawker Sea Hurricane Mk.IB

Code: **A05134**

Having proved itself during the savage dogfighting of the Battle of Britain, the Hawker Hurricane would also make a valuable contribution in protecting the vital sea lanes from German attack. Modified with the addition of catapult spools and a fuselage mounted arrester hook, Sea Hurricanes were embarked aboard Britain's diminutive aircraft carriers from mid 1941.

Available Now

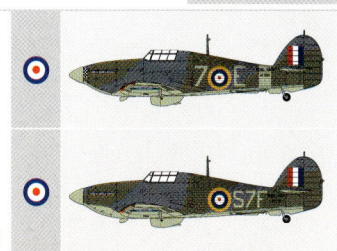

1:48 SCALE MILITARY AIRCRAFT

www.airfix.com

1:48 SCALE MILITARY AIRCRAFT

Hawker Sea Fury FB.11 'Export'

The last in an illustrious line of Hawker piston engined fighters, the Sea Fury entered service with the Royal Navy too late to see operations during WWII, but proved to be one of the fastest propeller driven aircraft ever produced. Attracting plenty of overseas interest, the Sea Fury was also operated in some numbers by the navies of Holland, Australia and Canada, with Australian Sea Fury's making a significant contribution to air operations during the Korean War.

Available Now — Code: **A06106**

Supermarine Spitfire F.Mk.22/24

Code: **A06101A**

As the final variants of the Spitfire to enter service, the Rolls-Royce Griffon powered Mk.22/24 were very different from the prototype aircraft that took to the sky in 1936. Double the weight and possessing more than twice the power, the last Spitfires had an increased climb rate of 80% over the prototype and were around 100mph faster.

Available Now

Junkers Ju87B-1 Stuka

Code: **A07114A**

Arguably one of the most distinctive aircraft of WWII, the Ju87B Stuka was a highly effective dive and attack bomber, capable of delivering precision bombing attacks, in support of the Germans 'Lightning War' concept. It also specifically employed the use of screaming sirens, designed to spread fear and panic amongst the enemy.

KIT INCLUDES 1 EXTRA SCHEME

Available April-19

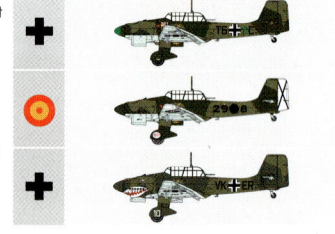

Junkers Ju87R-2/B-2 Stuka

Code: **A07115**

The Ju87B Stuka was also a highly effective maritime strike bomber. Capable of performing precision dive bombing attacks against any Allied vessel, the Stuka took a heavy toll of shipping in the English Channel, North Africa and in the Mediterranean. It also saw service with the air forces of Italy, Romania, Bulgaria and Hungary.

Available Now

English Electric Lightning F1/F1A/F3

Code: **A09179**

Used as the RAF's primary interceptor for more than two decades, the English Electric Lightning was the only all-British Mach 2 fighter aircraft. Powered by two Rolls-Royce Avon Turbojet engines, pilots often described it as "being saddled to a skyrocket". The Lightning retired from RAF service in the 1980s and was never required to shoot down a hostile aircraft.

Available Now

Please visit www.airfix.com/catalogue2019 to locate your nearest Airfix stockist

Hawker Hunter F.4

The service introduction of the Hawker Hunter F.4 in March 1955 presented the RAF with a more capable version of their sleek jet fighter, including a much needed increase in its internal fuel capacity. The F.4 also introduced the two distinctive streamlined chin blisters, which were designed to collect spent ammunition links from the guns, thus preventing potential damage to the aircraft.

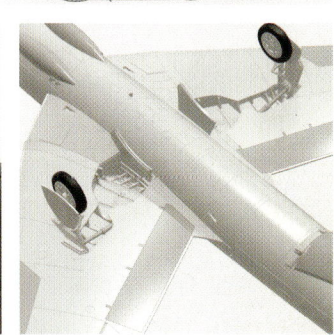

Available Nov-19 — Code: **A09189**

Hawker Hunter F.6

As far as classic British jet aircraft are concerned, few would argue that the beautiful Hawker Hunter should be placed at the head of this group, entering RAF service in 1954 and still providing training support almost 40 years later. The definitive interceptor version of the Hunter was the Mk.6 and by the end of 1958, all of the RAFs day fighter squadrons in Britain and Germany were equipped with these aircraft

Available Jan-19 — Code: **A09185**

Bristol Blenheim Mk.IF

Code: **A09186**

In September 1939, the RAF had more Bristol Blenheims in service than any other aircraft and it was to see extensive service during the savage air battles to come. Used mainly as a light bomber, the Blenheim was also developed into a long range fighter equipped with a ventral pack of four .303 machine guns, produced by the Ashford workshops of the Southern Railway.

Available Now

1:48 SCALE MILITARY AIRCRAFT

www.airfix.com

1:48 SCALE MILITARY AIRCRAFT

Gloster Meteor F.8
Code: **A09182**

Historically, the Gloster Meteor was Britain's first jet fighter and the only Allied jet aircraft to see service during the Second World War. The F.8 variant of the Meteor was perhaps the definitive incarnation of this famous aircraft and was the main RAF fighter throughout the 1950's, until superseded by the Hawker Hunter.

Available Now

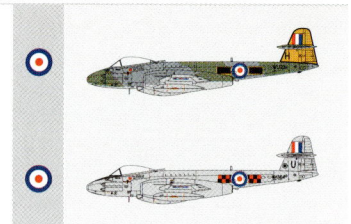

Gloster Meteor FR.9
Code: **A09188**

The Gloster Aircraft Company produced 126 Meteor FR.9s, modifying the existing Meteor F.8 design by fitting cameras in the nose alongside the guns, to produce a very effective armed reconnaissance aircraft. Used by the Royal Air Force during the 1950s in both West Germany and in Egypt to monitor the Suez Canal.

Available Now

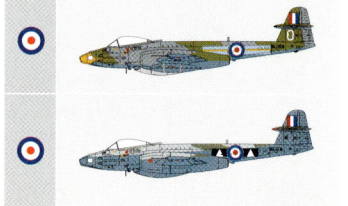

Gloster Meteor F.8 Korea
Code: **A09184**

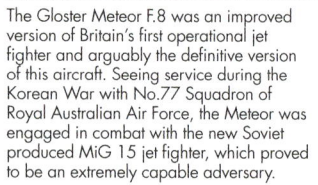

The Gloster Meteor F.8 was an improved version of Britain's first operational jet fighter and arguably the definitive version of this aircraft. Seeing service during the Korean War with No.77 Squadron of Royal Australian Air Force, the Meteor was engaged in combat with the new Soviet produced MiG 15 jet fighter, which proved to be an extremely capable adversary.

Available Now

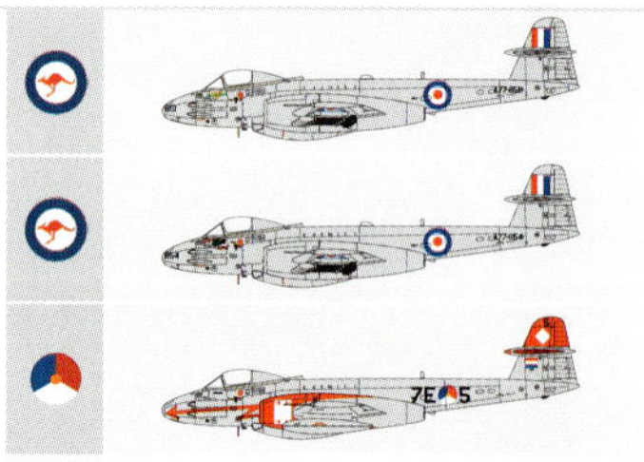

Supermarine Walrus Mk.1 'Silver Wings'
Code: **A09187**

The reputation of the Supermarine company was built on their ability to design and produce effective and reliable marine and amphibious aircraft for civilian and military use. The Walrus was a perfect example of their expertise and underlined the strength of the aircraft by performing a loop at the 1933 Hendon Air Pageant, to the astonishment of the spectators.

Available Now

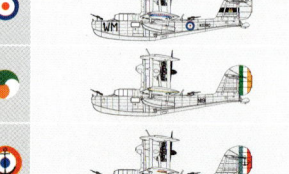

English Electric Canberra B(i).6/B.20
Code: **A10101A**

The incredible success of the English Electric Canberra jet bomber can be gauged by the length of time it remained in service with the Royal Air Force. With the first Canberras arriving at RAF No.101 Squadron in early 1951, the last photo-reconnaissance PR.9 machines were only withdrawn in 2006 – a remarkable 55 years in service.

Available Now

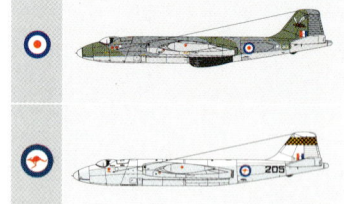

de Havilland Sea Vixen FAW.2
Code: **A11002**

RE-INTRODUCTION

The Sea Vixen represents the zenith of De Havilland's twin boom jet design philosophy. An all-weather fighter, the two-seat Sea Vixen was a capable design that served as a drone after its retirement from frontline service.

Available Jun-19

66

Please visit www.airfix.com/catalogue2019 to locate your nearest Airfix stockist

1:24 SCALE

This scale is perfect for those models where you want an expert level of detail.

NEW SCHEME
Hawker Typhoon Mk.1B 'Car Door'

KIT INCLUDES 1 EXTRA SCHEME

Hawker Typhoon Mk.1B 'Car Door'

These early machines were somewhat rushed into service and it was discovered that a number of modifications would be desirable, if not totally essential. Perhaps the most noticeable difference from the later models were around the canopy area – the first Typhoons were supplied with a forward opening 'car door' style cockpit entry for the pilot which even included a wind down window. The pilot also had a transparent roof panel, which hinged open to the left and some machines had the addition of a rear-facing mirror, on the canopy frame.

Available April-19 Code: A19003A

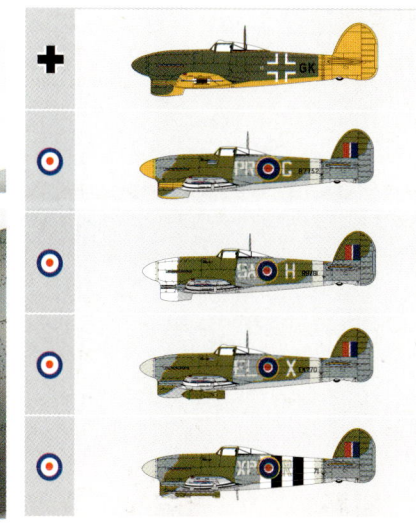

1:24 SCALE MILITARY AIRCRAFT

www.airfix.com

1:24 SCALE MILITARY AIRCRAFT

NEW MOULD Grumman F6F-5 Hellcat

- Over 500 parts
- Can be built with wings open or folded
- Includes full cockpit detail with open or closed canopy options
- Complete fully detailed radial engine, engine mount and all ancillaries
- Fully detailed gun bays with complete machine guns and ammunition trays
- Detailed undercarriage and undercarriage bays with options to build with wheels up or down

Please visit www.airfix.com/catalogue2019 to locate your nearest Airfix stockist

Grumman F6F-5 Hellcat

1:24   NEW MOULD   Available May-19   Code: **A19004**

Few aircraft in the history of aerial warfare can boast the impact and combat credentials of the Grumman F6F Hellcat, one of the finest fighting machines ever to take to the skies. A product of the already successful Grumman 'Ironworks', the company's design philosophy was only to produce aircraft which were easy to manufacture and maintain, and must be reliable in a combat situation. Importantly, it must be an excellent fighting machine and able to be mastered by the average wartime pilot following a standard conversion period. This no nonsense approach ensured that the Hellcat was ready to fight and available in some numbers when they eventually reached US Navy units in 1943.

Despite its combat introduction taking place relatively late in the war, the Hellcat would prove to be the 'mount of aces' and unquestionably ruled the skies of the Pacific Theatre. Posting some quite astonishing combat statistics, it has been reported that almost 75% of all aerial victories claimed by US Navy pilots were attributed to the Hellcat, which earned an impressive combat kill ratio of 19 to 1 in the Pacific Theatre. Although combat claims can be notoriously difficult to corroborate, this meant that on average, nineteen enemy aircraft were destroyed for the loss of a single Hellcat, a statistic which could not be bettered by any other combat aircraft in WWII. Perhaps the most impressive combat statistic earned by the Grumman Hellcat was that it made 'Aces' of no fewer than 305 US airmen, each one claiming five victories or more.

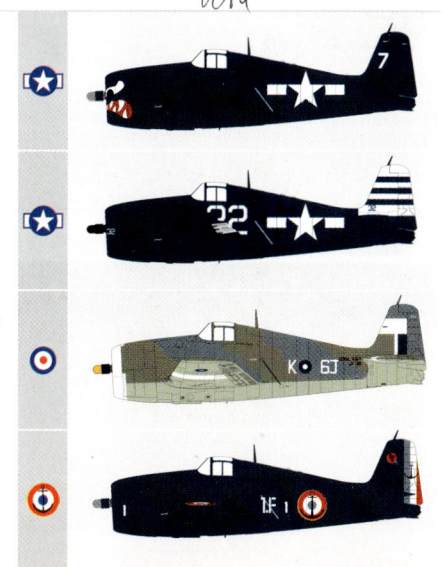

1:24 SCALE MILITARY AIRCRAFT

www.airfix.com

MILITARY VEHICLES

Bring your collection to life in 2019 with diorama figures and military vehicles from many different eras and countries.

Cromwell Mk.IV Cruiser Tank
Code: A02338

1:76

The Cromwell first saw action in 1944. Its crews succeeded in outflanking the heavier and more sluggish German tanks with superior speed, manoeuvrability and reliability.

Available Now

British Airborne Willys Jeep®
Code: A02339

1:72

The US Army's 4x4 was manufactured from 1941 to 1945. These small four-wheel drive utility vehicles are considered the iconic World War II utility vehicle, and inspired many similar light utility vehicles. They were able to carry and tow many loads, making for a highly manoeuvrable army.

Available Now

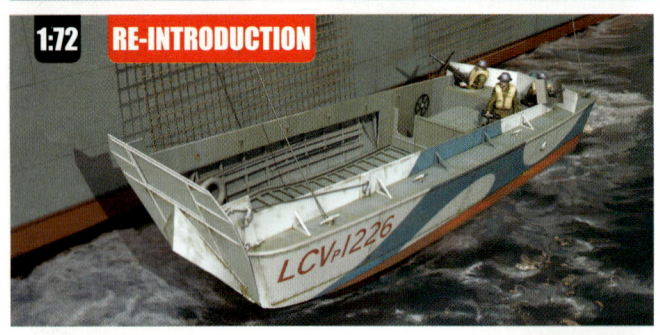

Higgins LCVP
Code: A02340

1:72 RE-INTRODUCTION

The Landing Craft, Vehicle, Personnel (LCVP) or Higgins boat was used extensively in amphibious landings in World War II. The craft was designed by Andrew Higgins of Louisiana, United States, based on boats made for operating in swamps and marshes. More than 20,000 were built, by Higgins Industries and licensees.

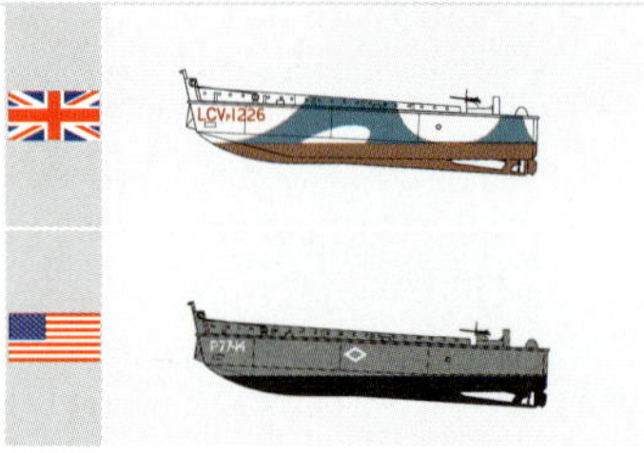

Available April-19

Bedford QLD/QLT Trucks
Code: A03306

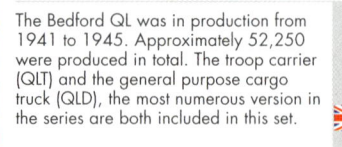

1:76 RE-INTRODUCTION

The Bedford QL was in production from 1941 to 1945. Approximately 52,250 were produced in total. The troop carrier (QLT) and the general purpose cargo truck (QLD), the most numerous version in the series are both included in this set.

Available April-19

17 Pdr Anti-Tank Gun
Code: A06361

1:32

The 17 PDR was an anti-tank gun capable of destroying the thickest German tank armour and was used in many theatres of war. Weighing in at just over 2,000 kg, it required at least seven crew to operate who were only partially protected by a flat, thick armoured shield.

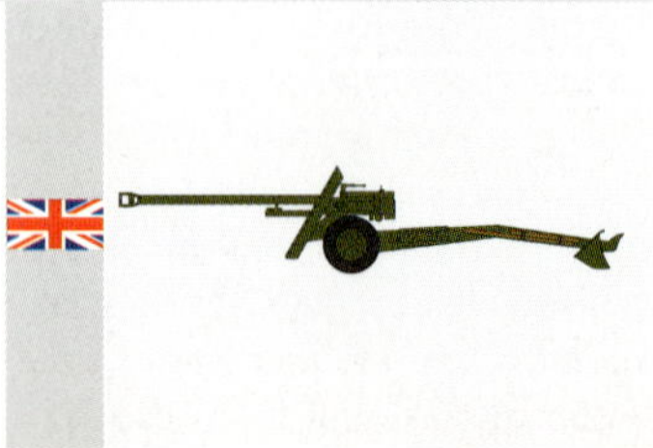

Available Now

Please visit www.airfix.com/catalogue2019 to locate your nearest Airfix stockist

1:35 SCALE

Introducing a new range of highly detailed tanks.

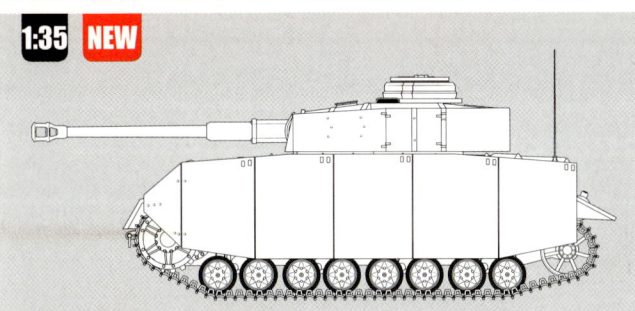

71

Panzer IV Ausf.H, Mid Version — Code: A1351

The German medium tank Panzerkampfwagen IV was developed in the late 1930s and was used extensively during WWII. The production of the Panzer IV Ausf. H started in June 1943. This version was designated the Sd. Kfz. 161/2. Compared to the previous variants, this model had Zimmerit paste on all the vertical surfaces of its armour in order to prevent adhesion of magnetic anti-tank mines. The turret roof was reinforced from 10mm to 16 and 25mm segments. 5mm hull skirts and 8mm turret skirts were added for further protection, which resulted in the elimination of the vision ports on the hull side. Later the hull was also fitted with triangular supports for the easily damaged side skirts. Along with some other modifications, these additions to the design increased the tank's weight to 25 tonnes, and the maximum speed dropped to 16 km/h on cross country terrain.

Available April 19

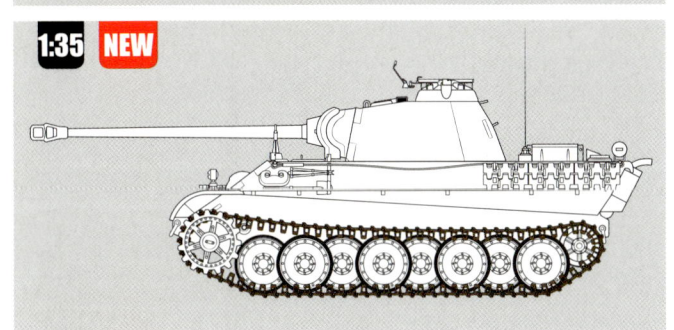

Panther Ausf.G — Code: A1352

On 3rd April 1944, M.A.N. reported that it had successfully completed trial production runs of the new Ausf.G chassis. M.A.N. built about 1143 Panther Ausf.G tanks between March 1944 and April 1945. Between July 1944 to March 1945 M.N.H. constructed 806 Panther Ausf.G tanks. Daimler-Benz finished 1004 Panther Ausf.G tanks between May 1944 and April 1945.
There were some minor differences between factory built tanks. M.N.H. fitted a cast steel Gleitschuh skid shoes instead of a rubber tire return roller behind the front track drive sprocket. The other two factories continued to fit rubber rimmed return rollers.

Available Dec 19

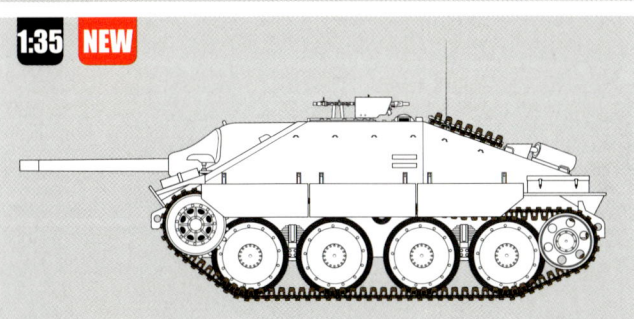

JagdPanzer 38 tonne Hetzer, Late Version — Code: A1353

The Jagdpanzer 38(t) (Sd.Kfz. 138/2), later known as Hetzer ("baiter"), was a German light tank destroyer of the Second World War based on a modified Czechoslovakian Panzer 38(t) chassis. The project was inspired by the Romanian "Maresal" tank destroyer. The name Hetzer was, at the time, not commonly used for this vehicle. It was the designation for a related prototype, the E-10. The Škoda factory confused the two names in its documentation for a short time and the very first unit equipped with the vehicle thus for a few weeks used the incorrect name until matters were cleared. However, there is a memorandum from Heinz Guderian to Hitler claiming that an unofficial name, Hetzer, had spontaneously been coined by the troops. Post-war historians made the name popular in their works, the vehicle was never named as such in official documents.

Available Oct 19

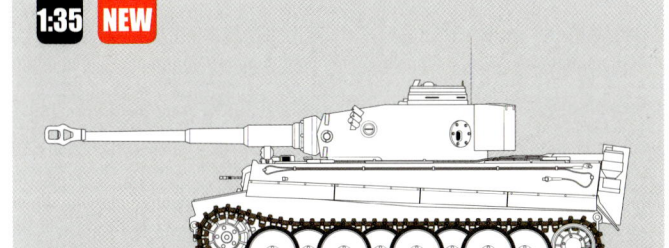

Tiger-1, Early Version - Operation Citadel — Code: A1354

Prochorovka is one of the best-known of the many battles on the Eastern Front during World War II. Tiger heavy tanks with deadly 88mm cannons, lumbered forward while hundreds of nimble Soviet T-34 medium tanks raced into the midst of the SS armour and threw the Germans into confusion. The Soviets closed with the Panzers, negating the Tigers' 88mm guns, outmanoeuvred the German armour and knocked out hundreds of German tanks. The Soviet tank force's audacious tactics resulted in a disastrous defeat for the Germans, and the disorganised SS divisions withdrew, leaving 400 destroyed tanks behind, including between 70 and 100 Tigers and many Panthers. Those losses smashed the SS divisions' fighting power, and as a result Hoth's Fourth Panzer Army had no chance to achieve even a partial victory in the south of the Soviet Union.

Available Oct 19

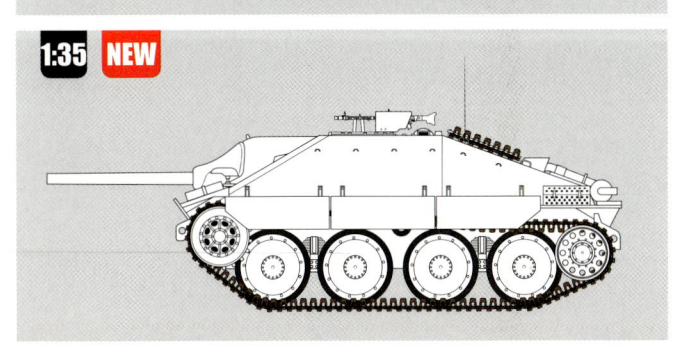

JagdPanzer 38 tonne Hetzer, Early Version — Code: A1355

The Jagdpanzer 38 (Sd.Kfz. 138/2), or Hetzer ("baiter"), was a WWII German light tank destroyer based on a modified Czechoslovakian Panzer 38(t) chassis. The Jagdpanzer 38 was more cost-effective than the ambitious Jagdpanther and Jagdtiger designs. Using a proven chassis, it avoided the mechanical problems of the larger armoured vehicles. It was built on the Panzerkampfwagen 38(t)'s widened and lengthened chassis with modified suspension (larger road-wheels from Praga TNH n.A prototype reconnaissance tank) and up-rated engine. The new engine was 160 PS Praga AC/2 6-cylinder engine controlled by Praga-Wilson gearbox (5 forward and 1 reverse gear). Chassis was modified in order to accommodate larger gun and thicker armour than regular Panzerkampfwagen 38(t) tank. Its combat weight was 16 metric tons and could travel at maximum speed of some 42 km/h.

Available June 19

1:35 SCALE MILITARY VEHICLES

www.airfix.com

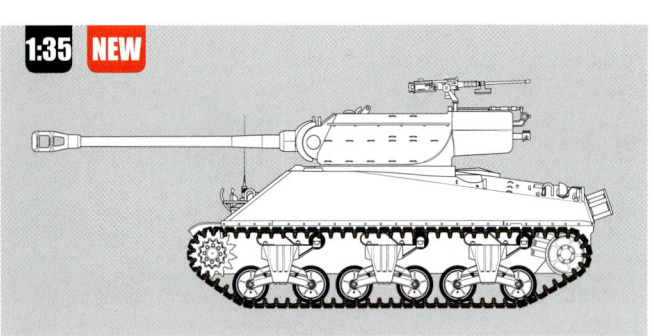

1:35 SCALE MILITARY VEHICLES

M36B1 GMC (U.S. Army)
Code: **A1356**

The M36 tank destroyer, formally 90 mm Gun Motor Carriage, M36, was an American tank destroyer used during World War II. The M36 combined the hull of the M10 tank destroyer, which used the M4 Sherman's reliable chassis and drivetrain, combined with sloped armour. Conceived in 1943, the M36 first served in combat in Europe in October 1944, where it partially replaced the M10 tank destroyer. However when coming up against the heaviest tanks of the Wehrmacht at the end of that year, the need for 90 mm gunned tank destroyers became urgent and during October–December 1944, 187 conversions of standard Medium Tank M4A3 hulls were produced by Grand Blanc Arsenal. These vehicles, designated M36B1, were rushed to the European Theatre of Operations and used in combat alongside standard M36s.

Available Aug 19

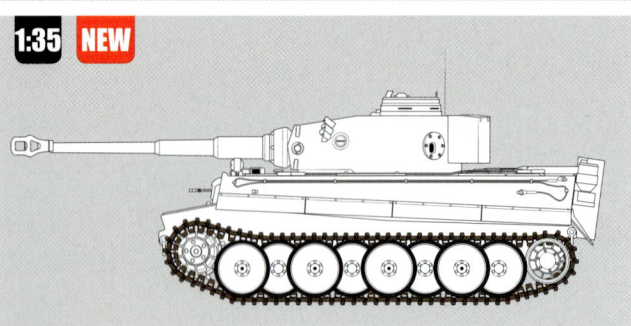

Tiger 1, Early Production Version
Code: **A1357**

Production of the Tiger I began in August 1942 and 1,355 had been built by August 1944 when production ceased. It took about twice as long to build a Tiger I as another German tank of the period. Hitler ordered the vehicle be pressed into service months earlier than planned. A platoon of four Tigers went into action on 23rd September 1942 near Leningrad. Operating in swampy, forested terrain, their movement was largely confined to roads and tracks, making defence against them far easier. These early models were plagued by problems with the transmission which had difficulty handling the great weight of the vehicle if pushed too hard. Many broke down. One of the Tigers from this engagement became stuck in swampy ground and had to be abandoned. Captured largely intact, it enabled the Soviets to study the design and prepare countermeasures.

Available Aug 19

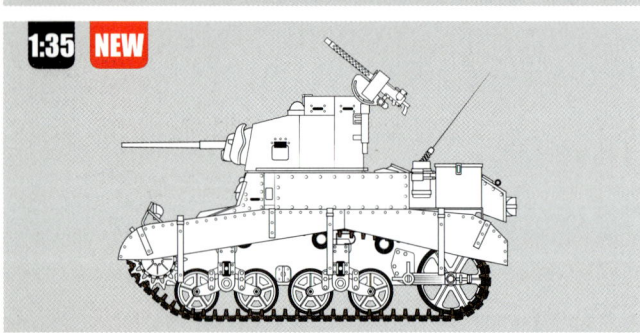

M3 Stuart, Honey (British Version)
Code: **A1358**

The M3's ability to "shoot and scoot" as well as keeping the crew safe from small fire arms fire, earned an affectionate nickname of "Honey". Easy to maintain, it traveled 10 to 20 mph faster than the British or enemy tanks. The M3 had thicker armour, a lengthened hull, and a trailer idler wheel to improve weight distribution. The turret had three pistol ports and shortened recoil mechanism. The 37mm M6 gun was adequate early in the war, but by 1942, the German counterparts surpassed the M3's range. The narrow width of the M3 could not accommodate a larger gun. The M3A1 was fitted with a Westinghouse gyrostabilizer, a turret basket and an oil gear hydraulic traverse mechanism, but lacked a turret cupola. The earlier version, the Stuart III, was powered by Continental W-970-9A-7 cylinder radial gas 250 hp engine, but by mid-1941, the Stuart IVs used a Guiberson T-1020 air cooled radial diesel engine.

Available Feb 19

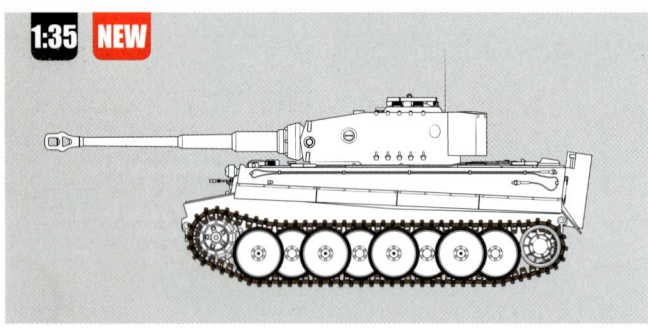

Tiger-1, Mid Version
Code: **A1359**

The tank was given its nickname "Tiger" by Ferdinand Porsche, and the Roman numeral was added after the later Tiger II entered production. Tiger I was a German heavy tank of World War II deployed from 1942 in Africa and Europe, usually in independent heavy tank battalions. Its final designation was Panzerkampfwagen VI Tiger Ausf. E often shortened to Tiger. The Tiger I gave the Wehrmacht its first armoured fighting vehicle that mounted the 8.8 cm KwK 36 gun. 1,347 were built between August 1942 and August 1944. It carried a crew of 5 (driver, radio operator, gunner, commander and loader), and was powered by a water-cooled V-12 engine, taking to speeds up to 28 m.p.h. (45 k.m.p.h.), and along with its feared main weapon carried two 7.92mm MG-34 machine guns, used in close combat situations.

Available June 19

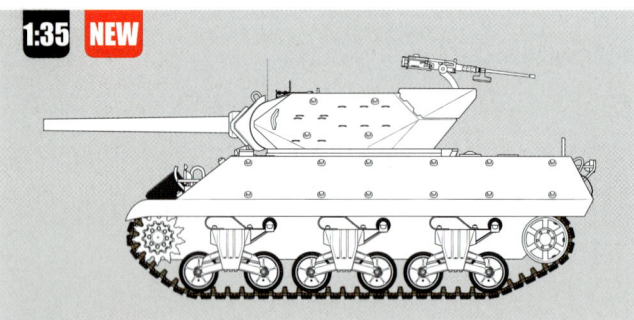

M10 GMC (U.S. Army)
Code: **A1360**

The prototype of the M10 was developed in early 1942, and was delivered in April of that year. After requested changes to the hull and turret, the modified version was readied for production in June 1943, appearing as the 3-inch Gun Motor Carriage M10. It mounted a 3-inch (76.2 mm) Gun M7 in a rotating turret on a modified M4A2 Sherman tank chassis. Productions ran from September 1942 to December 1943. The M10 was numerically the most important U.S. tank destroyer of World War II, combining thin but sloped armor with the M4 Sherman's reliable drivetrain and a reasonably potent anti-tank weapon mounted in an open-topped turret. Despite its obsolescence in the face of more powerful German tanks like the Panther and the introduction of more powerful and better-designed types as replacements, the M10 remained in service until the end of the war.

Available April 19

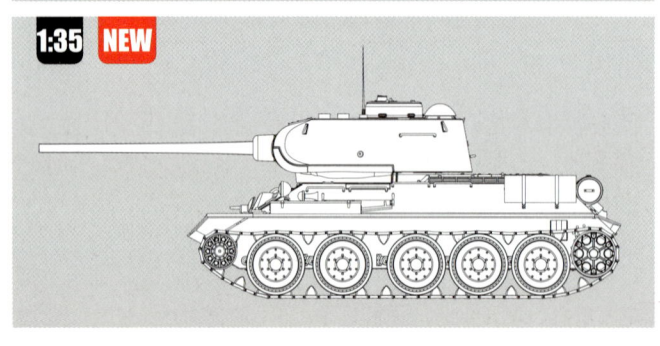

T34/85, 112 Factory Production
Code: **A1361**

When the first T-34-85s (85mm gun) delivered by Zavod #112 appeared, they were given to the best units, the elite Red Guards battalions. However, they were in training during December 1943, so it is uncertain whether they saw action before January or February 1944. By then, around 400 had already been delivered to front-line units and instantly became popular with the crews. They gradually replaced the T-34/76 and in mid-1944 the T-34-85 outnumbered the older versions. By then they formed the bulk of the tank units on the eve of Operation Bagration, the Soviet response to the Allied landings in Normandy, and the biggest offensive ever planned by the Red Army to date. This was the final push, aimed at Berlin. Before the production built-up, the T-34-85 model 1943 were usually given to chosen crews, usually of the Guard units.

Available June 19

Please visit www.airfix.com/catalogue2019 to locate your nearest Airfix stockist

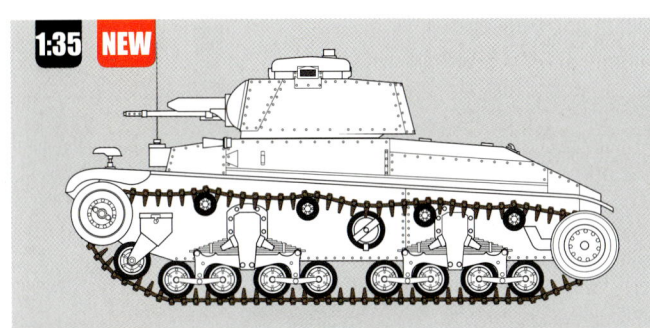

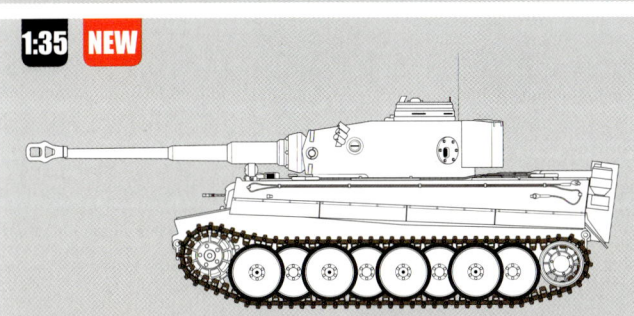

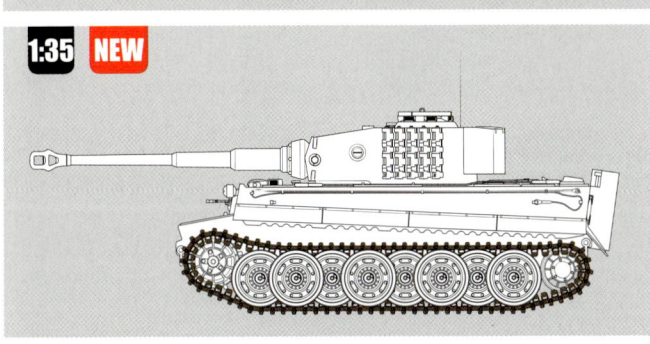

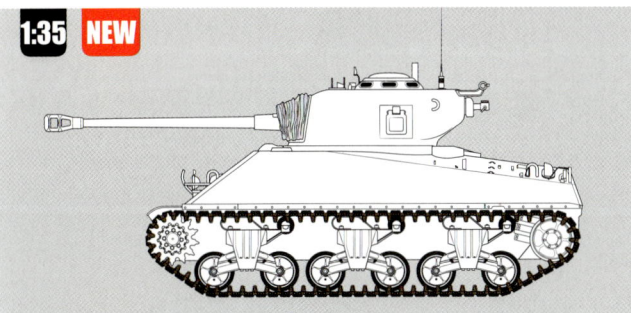

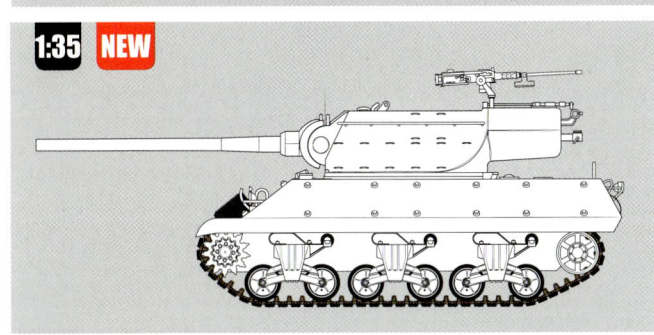

German Light Tank Pz.Kpfw.35(t) — Code: A1362

The Panzerkampfwagen 35(t), shortened to Panzer 35(t) or abbreviated as Pz.Kpfw. 35(t), was a Czechoslovakian designed light tank used mainly by Nazi Germany during World War II. The letter (t) stood for tschechisch (German: "Czech"). In Czechoslovakian service it had the formal designation Lehký tank vzor 35 (Light Tank Model 35), but was commonly referred to as the LT vz. 35 or LT-35. A total of 434 were built; of these, the Germans seized 244 when they occupied Bohemia-Moravia in March 1939 and the Slovaks acquired 52 when they declared independence from Czechoslovakia at the same time. Others were exported to Bulgaria and Romania. In German service, it saw combat during the early years of WW II, notably the invasion of Poland, the Battle of France and the invasion of the Soviet Union before being retired or sold off in 1942.

Available Feb 19

Tiger-1, Early Version — Code: A1363

Production of the Tiger I began in August 1942 and 1,355 had been built by August 1944 when production ceased. It took about twice as long to build a Tiger I as another German tank of the period. Hitler ordered the vehicle be pressed into service months earlier than planned. A platoon of four Tigers went into action on 23rd September 1942 near Leningrad. Operating in swampy, forested terrain, their movement was largely confined to roads and tracks, making defence against them far easier. These early models were plagued by problems with the transmission which had difficulty handling the great weight of the vehicle if pushed too hard. Many broke down. One of the Tigers from this engagement became stuck in swampy ground and had to be abandoned. Captured largely intact, it enabled the Soviets to study the design and prepare countermeasures.

Available Oct 19

Tiger-1, Late Version — Code: A1364

During the whole of its service history, the Tiger-1 was constantly improved upon and adapted to counter the ever-improving Allied tanks and firepower it found itself up against.
This version from the summer of 1944 comes with a asymmetric turret, 88mm cannon, mantlet, engine deck and accessory pack. A Zimmerit tool is also included.

Available April 19

M4A3(76)W, Battle of the Bulge — Code: A1365

The Chrysler Corporation began producing the M4A3(76) in March 1944. Many of their first units arrived almost simultaneously in France & Italy in August 1944. It, like all the Shermans, saw a steady flow of minor improvements, and versions of this tank with HVSS (horizontal volute spring suspension) started arriving in December of 1944, just prior to the Axis push into the Ardennes region, and would become increasingly common from that point on as replacement tanks entered the combat zone. These tanks were very well received, the Ford GAA was a very good engine for a tank in the Sherman's weight range. The low RPM the motor matched the existing gear ratios in the transmission, and the motor more than a match for the stresses most operations put it under. Once the HVSS suspension versions began replacing previous tanks, this really became the ultimate Sherman.

Available Oct 19

M36/M36B2, Battle of the Bulge — Code: A1366

The M36 was introduced to replace the M10 which only had a 76mm gun. The M36 had a 90mm gun with greater armour piercing capability. In the Battle of the Bulge in December 1944, it gave it the capability of combating the Tigers and Panthers of the Wehrmacht. The M36 with its new turret was placed on converted M10A1 hulls. The M36B2 used the same turret but was placed on the M4A2 hulls which had a diesel engine. They both had a long service life, particularly in other nations services.

Available Aug 19

U.S. Tractor — Code: A1367

During 1941 to 1945 over 15,000 specially built and designed military tractors were built in the U.S. Approximately 40 variants were produced and were used in every theatre the U.S. forces operated in. One interesting fact was that the manual for this military tractor included instructions for destroying the tractor should it be in danger of being seized by the enemy.
Many of them stayed in both military and civilian use long after the war.

Available Mar 19

1:48 / 1:72 / 1:76 SCALE RUINED RESIN BUILDINGS

RUINED RESIN BUILDINGS

Ready-made resin buildings, fully detailed damage, suitable to be painted with Humbrol enamels or acrylics.

Glazing included with selected buildings.

1:48

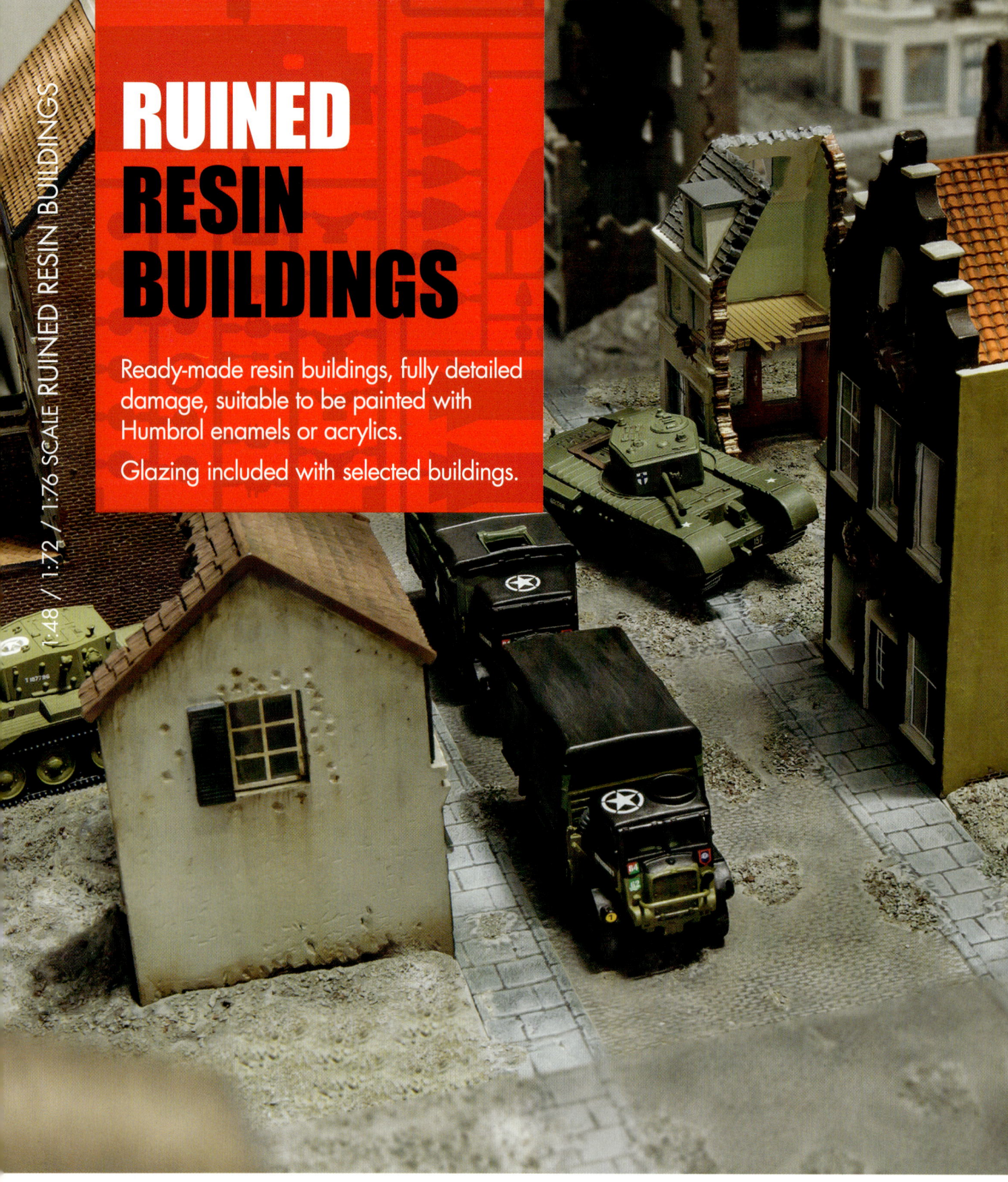

Afghan Single Storey House

Code: **A75010**

A slightly larger house of a typical Afghan design to enable the fantastic range of Airfix Afghanistan models come to life. As with the first house there is space inside to place figures to further enhance the modelling possibilities.

Available Now

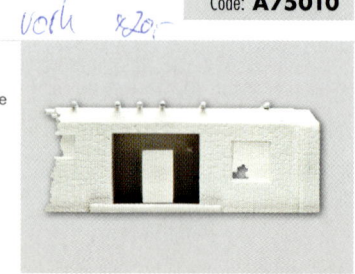

Please visit www.airfix.com/catalogue2019 to locate your nearest Airfix stockist

Narrow Road Bridge Broken Span

Code: **A75012**

Attacking and bombing bridges across Europe was a strategic necessity throughout WWII and this model represents a typical ruined example that makes for excellent possibilities for modelling superb dioramas as well as wargaming features.

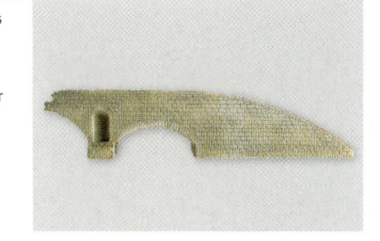

Available Now

Italian Farmhouse

Code: **A75013**

1943 saw the Allies invading what was still a hostile Italy, and this farmhouse is typical of those found across south and central parts. The three stories and steps make for plenty of diorama and gaming opportunities.

Available Now

Italian Townhouse

Code: **A75014**

During the fierce battles in the narrow streets of many Italian towns, buildings like this were bombarded by both sides to try and extract dug-in troops.

Available Now

Polish Bank

Code: **A75015**

Poland was attacked by Nazi Germany in September 1939, and this invasion sparked the start of World War II. The destruction caused by this and the later Soviet counter offensives during 1944 and 1945 meant many important buildings were ruined. This bank building typifies this destruction.

Available Now

Czech Restaurant

Code: **A75016**

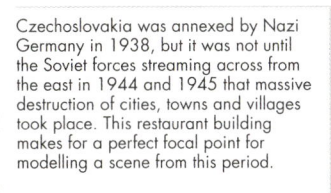

Czechoslovakia was annexed by Nazi Germany in 1938, but it was not until the Soviet forces streaming across from the east in 1944 and 1945 that massive destruction of cities, towns and villages took place. This restaurant building makes for a perfect focal point for modelling a scene from this period.

Available Now

European City Steps

Code: **A75017**

These city steps enable a huge scope of modelling opportunities to be created, and these types of steps are to be found right across Europe. Great to be used in wargaming scenarios too 1:76, 1:72 and even larger scale figures can be used with these.

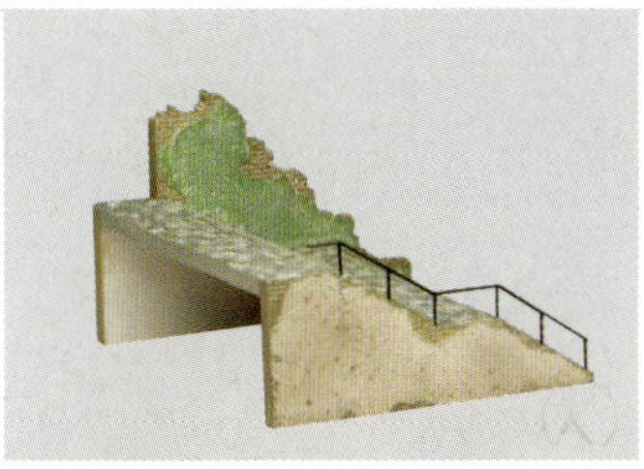

Available Now

www.airfix.com

1:72 SCALE VINTAGE CLASSICS

AIRFIX
VINTAGE CLASSICS

AIRCRAFT
FIESELER STORCH

Enjoy the nostalgia with our revival of classic models. The boxes feature original paintings by an impressive range of artists.

Fieseler Storch

1:72 RE-INTRODUCTION Code: A01047V

Mould Tools made in 1967, pack illustration by Roy Cross, 1967. One of the great Luftwaffe aircraft of the Second World War, the ungainly looking Fieseler Storch may not have commanded the same respect as the fast and agile Messerschmitt Bf 109 fighter, yet its low speed handling and short field performance was without equal. Entering Luftwaffe service in 1937, the Storch performed the vital roles of Army cooperation, liaison and reconnaissance, meaning the aircraft was never too far away from the front lines and didn't always need to be flown there. Designed to allow the high mounted wings to fold back in a similar manner to how aircraft are stored on ships, the Storch could either be loaded on a train, or simply towed behind a suitable vehicle, as they headed towards the action. The high wing and unobstructed cockpit meant that the pilot and his observer had an unrivalled view of the battlefield situation below and the aircraft's low speed made it extremely difficult for opposition fighters to shoot it down. Used extensively by Rommel during the ebb and flow of the North African Campaign, the Storch had an incredible stall speed of just 31mph and if flying in to a headwind with wing slats and flaps deployed, it almost had the ability to hover. Perhaps the most famous use of a Storch was when one was used to rescue a surrounded Benito Mussolini from a remote, rocky mountain top, landing in less than 100 feet and taking off again in only a slightly longer distance, the only fixed wing aircraft capable of doing so.

Available Sept-19

Please visit www.airfix.com/catalogue2019 to locate your nearest Airfix stockist

Hawker Demon

Mould Tools made in 1957, pack illustration by James Goulding, 1989. The period between the First and Second World Wars was something of a golden era for British aviation and saw the introduction of some of the most attractive aircraft to see RAF service. With their gleaming silver fuselages and bright squadron markings, many of these aircraft also represented the absolute pinnacle of biplane aviation technology. The introduction of the Hawker Hart light bomber proved to be something of an embarrassment for the RAF, as it was faster than the current fighter aircraft in service. The answer to this problem was simple, ask Hawker Aviation to build a fighter version of their Hart. Powered by the mighty Rolls Royce Kestrel engine, the new two seat 'Hart Fighter' proved to be a great success and even though it was quickly renamed Demon to differentiate between the two aircraft, just over 300 of these elegant fighters would eventually be produced. Unfortunately, this golden era for biplanes occurred just as the first monoplane designs were being developed and their reign would prove to be a short, if glorious one. Just as the Demon had been introduced to combat a new breed of fast biplane bombers, so the performance of the new Bristol Blenheim would render it obsolete as a fighter almost overnight.

Available Sept-19 Code: **A01052V**

Bristol Bulldog

Mould Tools made in 1969, pack illustration by Roy Cross, 1969. The handsome Bristol Bulldog was without doubt one of the most important RAF aircraft of the inter-war period. Introduced in 1929, the strong and manoeuvrable Bulldog was Britain's main front line single seat fighter at a time when aviation was all about style and grace, and was flown by the nations most talented young airmen. One of these young pilots was Douglas Bader, a gifted airman with a flair for aerobatics but something of a daredevil reputation. Whilst performing unauthorised low level aerobatics in his Bulldog fighter, the wing of his aircraft clipped the ground sending it tumbling across the airfield. Bader was seriously injured and only survived thanks to the expertise of the surgeons at the Royal Berkshire Hospital. Suffering a double amputation of his shattered legs, the story of Bader's recovery and subsequent struggle to re-join the Royal Air Force made him a national hero and one of the most famous fighter pilots of the Second World War. By the time he was flying Spitfires from RAF Duxford, the Bristol Bulldog had long since been withdrawn from front line service, with just a few examples soldiering on in a secondary training role. Only two of these beautiful aircraft are known to have survived.

Available Sept-19 Code: **A01055V**

Henschel Hs123A-1

Mould Tools made in 1970, pack illustration by Roy Cross, 1970. As you might expect from a new aircraft manufacturer previously involved in the production of railway locomotives, the Henschel Hs123 biplane attack aircraft was as tough as they come. Intended as a dive bomber and close air support aircraft, the Hs123 performed well during its combat introduction in the Spanish Civil War, however, its lack of range and relatively small bomb load saw future development suppressed due to the impending introduction of the monoplane Ju-87 Stuka. Despite this setback, the aircraft still in service at the start of WWII were sent into action, with its pilots perfecting the art of close air support for advancing ground units. Proving to be extremely rugged, these agile little biplanes could absorb significant levels of damage, pressing home their attacks and bringing their pilots home safely. Serving through the Blitzkrieg attacks against Poland, France and the Low Countries, the Hs123 would come into its own during the savage fighting on the Eastern Front, where aircraft would be based close to the front lines, flying several offensive sorties each day. The aircraft proved so effective, that they were only withdrawn from service in the spring of 1944 and only then due to a lack of serviceable aircraft and spares.

Available Sept-19 Code: **A02051V**

1:72 / 1:44 SCALE VINTAGE CLASSICS

de Havilland Heron MkII
Code: A03001V

Mould Tools made in 1959, pack illustration by Mike Renwick, 1993. Building on the success of de Havilland's earlier twin engined Dove small passenger aircraft, the company's attempt to produce a slightly larger airliner resulted in the first flight of the Heron in May 1950. Capable of comfortably carrying 17 passengers, the Heron had a longer fuselage and wings than its predecessor and employed an additional pair of Gipsy Queen engines, providing reassurance for crew and passengers alike. Early models of the aircraft were produced with a fixed undercarriage, but the Mk.II variant introduced a number of upgrades, most noticeably being the adoption of a retractable undercarriage, with the resultant reduction in drag. Although only 150 were built, Heron's served with both the RAF and Royal Navy.

Available Oct-19

Hawker Siddeley Dominie T.1
Code: A03009V

During the 1960s and 70s, the sheer variety of aircraft in service with the Royal Air Force must have made this an incredible time to be either a pilot or an aviation enthusiast. Providing the RAF with a capable air engineer, navigation and weapons system operations trainer, the distinguished looking Hawker Siddeley Dominie T.1 started life as one of the world's first practical executive business jets, with its speed and cabin space making it an ideal candidate for military service. Used to train crews destined for Britain's V bomber force, or the maritime patrol Nimrod, the Dominie would prove to be one of the RAF's most useful aircraft types and was only withdrawn from service in January 2011.

Available Oct-19

Handley Page Jetstream
Code: A03012V

The Handley Page Jetstream was a sleek twin engined turboprop aircraft designed as a regional airliner specifically to satisfy the lucrative US market. The Jetstream offered great promise, especially when an order for 20 aircraft was placed, even before the design drawings had been completed. Re-engining the aircraft with a US Garrett TPE-331 turboprop powerplant resulted in a significant order from the USAF, but this was subsequently cancelled, due to late delivery. Spiralling costs resulted in the bankruptcy of Handley Page, however, production of the Jetstream was taken over by Scottish Aviation and the Jetstream would go on to serve as the RAF's standard multi-engined pilot trainer for many years and later as an observer trainer with the Royal Navy.

Available Oct-19

Northrop P-61 Black Widow
Code: A04006V

One of the most distinctive aircraft of the Second World War, the P-61 Black Widow was the first US aircraft designed specifically for combat at night and the first developed with radar as its primary method of target detection. Powered by two mighty Pratt & Whitney Double Wasp engines, this was a very big aeroplane for a fighter, but if it managed to detect an enemy aircraft, its impressive array of offensive firepower would usually result in the Black Widow living up to its sinister name. It is thought that a P-61 Black Widow operating in the Pacific Theatre scored the final Allied aerial victory of the Second World War, in the hours just prior to Japan's surrender.

Available Nov-19

Savoia-Marchetti SM79
Code: A04007V

The Savoia-Marchetti SM79 'Sparrowhawk' was Italy's main medium bomber of the Second World War and one of the most effective bombers operated by Axis forces. With its unusual three engined configuration, the SM79 was a fast aeroplane, possessing endurance, which made it especially effective in operations over the Mediterranean. As a torpedo bomber, the SM79 earned a reputation for being one of the best anti-shipping aircraft of WWII and should the aircraft have to land on water as a result of damage sustained during an attack, the wooden wings and fabric covered fuselage gave the crew ample time to take to their life rafts. After the armistice with Italy, around 36 'Sparrowhawks' continued to fight with the Germans, some wearing Luftwaffe markings.

Available Nov-19

Concorde
Code: A05170V

Without doubt one of the most famous aircraft in the history of aviation, the Anglo-French BAC/SUD (later BAe/Aerospatiale) Concorde was a supersonic transport aircraft which possessed performance that would put most military fighters to shame. With two prototype aircraft built to prove the viability of supersonic flight for the civilian market, the British Concorde 002 (G-BSST) made its first flight from Filton on 9th April 1969 and joined its French counterpart at the Paris Airshow later the same year, where they both made their debuts. Ultimately, only Air France and British Airways would operate Concorde commercially and even though only 20 aircraft were built, they always represented the ultimate way to fly and a blue riband service for the rich and famous.

Available Sept-19

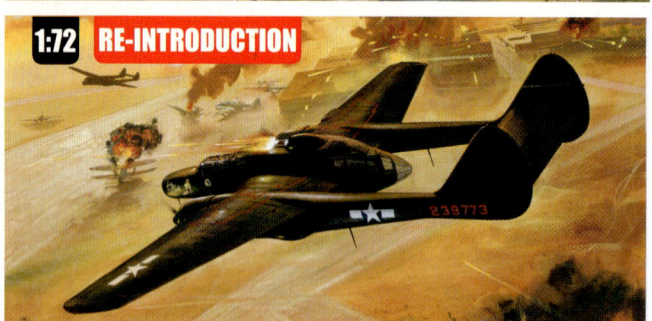

Please visit www.airfix.com/catalogue2019 to locate your nearest Airfix stockist

AIRFIX

VINTAGE CLASSICS

MILITARY VEHICLES
TIGER TANK Page 82

1:76 RE-INTRODUCTION

Matilda 'Hedgehog'

Based on the British Matilda tank it was fitted with a 7 spigot 'Hedgehog' naval mortar. The launcher folded horizontal, facing forward for travel, then could be raised up to 80 degrees for firing. It fired forward over the turret. Not being traversable, the driver had to aim the vehicle at the target.

Available Sept-19   Code: **A02335V**

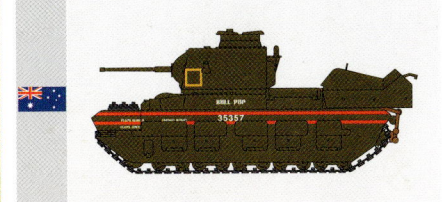

1:76 SCALE VINTAGE CLASSICS

www.airfix.com

1:76 SCALE VINTAGE CLASSICS

WWI Female Tank

The 'Female' version of the MkI tank was produced in larger numbers than it's 'Male' partner, this was due to the four Vickers machine guns mounted on the sides, which were more effective in combat than the heavier guns carried by the 'Male' tank in the treacherous conditions on the Western Front.

Available Sept-19   Code: **A02337V**

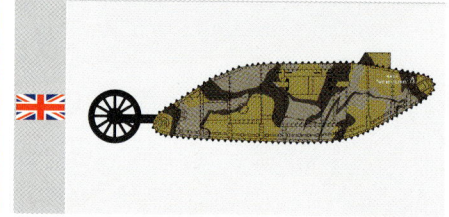

WWI Male Tank Mk.I

Mould Tools made in 1967, pack illustration by Roy Cross, 1967. On the 15th September 1916 at Flers-Courcelette a new weapon appeared on the battlefield of the Western Front – the tank. The 'male' version carried two 6-pdr naval guns and 4 Hotchkiss machine guns.

Available Now   Code: **A01315V**

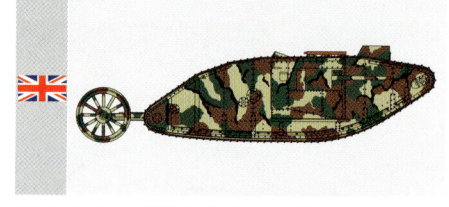

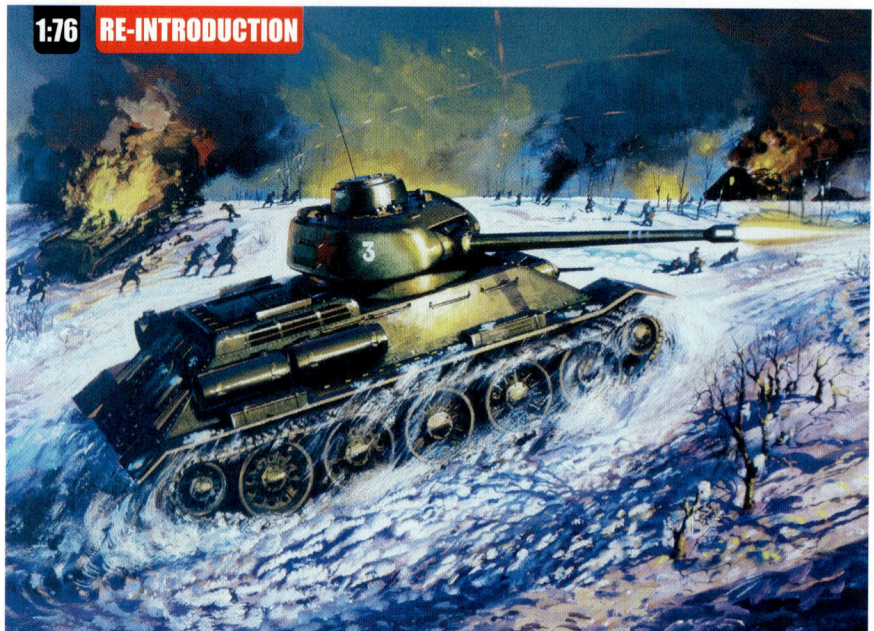

Russian T34

Mould Tools made in 1968, pack illustration by Roy Cross. The T-34 was arguably by for the best tank design in WWII. In addition to having an excellent combination of firepower, armour, mobility and shape, its superb technical design emphasised simplicity and durability making it possible to mass produce it in large numbers and gave it a very high field and combat reliability.

Available Now   Code: **A01316V**

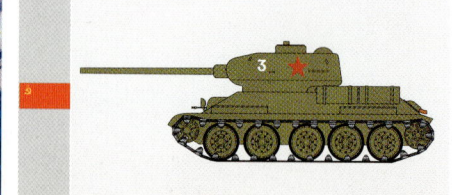

Please visit www.airfix.com/catalogue2019 to locate your nearest Airfix stockist

AIRFIX VINTAGE CLASSICS
D DAY TANKS

This range comes in vintage style packaging with classic illustrations. Bring your D-Day diorama to life with these beautifully detailed tanks.

Sherman M4 Mk1
Code: **A01303V**

1:76 RE-INTRODUCTION

The M4 Sherman was the primary tank used by the Allies during World War II. Thousands were also distributed via lend-lease, including the British Commonwealth and Soviet armies. Britain named the M4 (Mki) after General William Tecumsen Sherman, who fought with great distinction and bravery in the American Civil War.

Available May-19

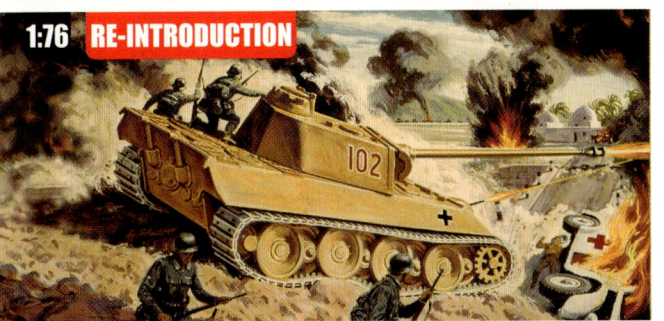

Panther
Code: **A01302V**

1:76 RE-INTRODUCTION

Mould Tools made in 1961, pack Illustration by G. Schule, 1961. Developed initially to counter the Russian T-34, the Panther was sent to frontline units in the spring of 1943, and first saw major combat at Kursk. With the correction of the production related mechanical difficulties, the Panther became highly popular with German tankers and a fearsome weapon on the battlefield.

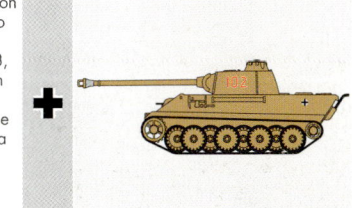

Available Now

Churchill Mk.VII
Code: **A01304V**

1:76 RE-INTRODUCTION

Mould Tools made in 1961, pack Illustration by Ron Jobson, 1975. The Churchill was the standard British infantry tank from 1941. It was not fast but had heavy armour, good firepower and good cross-country performance. The Mk.VII used a 75mm gun and had increased frontal armour. It first saw service in Normandy in 1944.

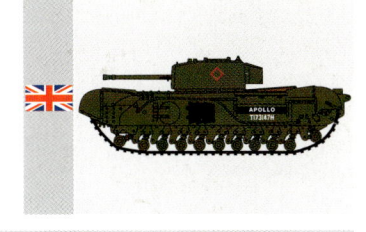

Available Now

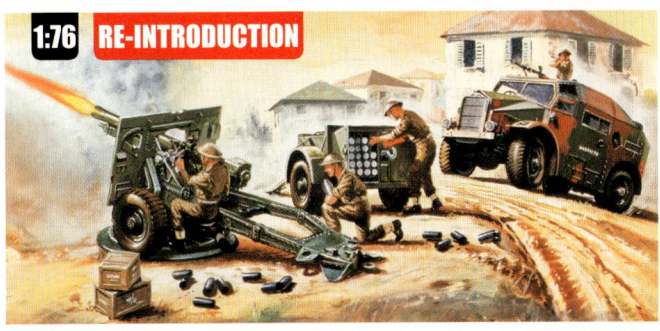

25PDR Field Gun & Quad
Code: **A01305V**

1:76 RE-INTRODUCTION

Mould Tools made in 1963, pack illustration by Roy Cross, 1964. Generally thought to be one of the best field guns of WWII, the 25pdr saw service throughout the conflict with British and Commonwealth forces. For transport the gun and limber were towed behind a Morris Commercial C8 FAT Quad.

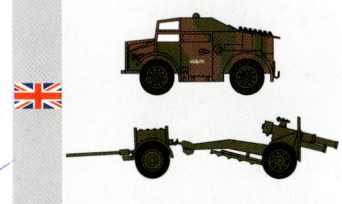

Available Now

Stug III 75mm Assault Gun
Code: **A01306V**

1:76 RE-INTRODUCTION

Mould Tools made in 1962, pack illustration by G. Schule, 1963. The Sturmgeschutz (Stug) III was a turretless tank on a Panzer III chassis which enabled it to carry a formidable 75mm high velocity gun. It was used extensively in all theatres of WWII.

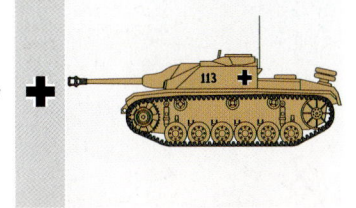

Available Now

www.airfix.com

1:76 SCALE VINTAGE CLASSICS

1:76 RE-INTRODUCTION

Tiger 1
Code: **A01308V**

The Tiger I was produced from late 1942 as an answer to the formidable Soviet armour encountered in the initial months of Operation Barbarossa. The Tiger I design gave the Wehrmacht its first tank mounting the 88mm gun. During the course of the war, the Tiger I saw combat on all German battlefronts.

Available May-19

1:76 RE-INTRODUCTION

Bren Gun Carrier & 6PDR Anti-Tank Gun
Code: **A01309V**

Mould Tools made in 1964, pack illustration by G. Schule, 1966. First employed in North Africa in 1942, the 6-pounder anti-tank gun was able to destroy all German tanks then in service. It was usually towed by a Universal or 'Bren' Carrier.

Available Now

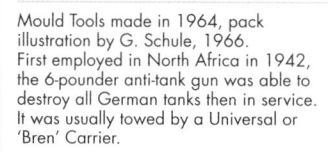

1:76 RE-INTRODUCTION

SdKfz.234 Armoured Car
Code: **A01311V**

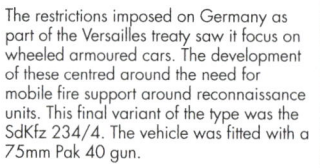

The restrictions imposed on Germany as part of the Versailles treaty saw it focus on wheeled armoured cars. The development of these centred around the need for mobile fire support around reconnaissance units. This final variant of the type was the SdKfz 234/4. The vehicle was fitted with a 75mm Pak 40 gun.

Available May-19

1:76 RE-INTRODUCTION

AEC Matador & 5.5inch Gun
Code: **A01314V**

Mould Tools made in 1966, pack illustration by Ken McDonough, 1978. The 5.5 inch gun first went into service with the Royal Artillery in North Africa in 1941 and was pulled by the famous four-wheel drive AEC Matador. The gun was handled by a team of ten men and fired an 82lb shell.

Available Now

1:76 RE-INTRODUCTION

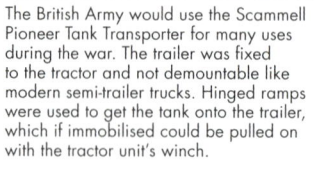

Scammell Tank Transporter
Code: **A02301V**

The British Army would use the Scammell Pioneer Tank Transporter for many uses during the war. The trailer was fixed to the tractor and not demountable like modern semi-trailer trucks. Hinged ramps were used to get the tank onto the trailer, which if immobilised could be pulled on with the tractor unit's winch.

Available May-19

1:76 RE-INTRODUCTION

Buffalo Amphibian & Jeep®
Code: **A02302V**

This landing vehicle was designed for the US Army, and later used by the British Army. This box also contains a 4X4 Utility Truck. Although usually associated with the Pacific theatre, toward the end of the war LVTs were employed in Europe as well.

Available May-19

Please visit www.airfix.com/catalogue2019 to locate your nearest Airfix stockist

88mm Gun & Tractor
Code: **A02303V**

1:76 RE-INTRODUCTION

Mould Tools made in 1967, pack illustration by Roy Cross, 1967. The "88" proved to be an excellent anti-tank gun in France in 1940. By the time it arrived in North Africa it was a feared tank killer, which could knock out any Allied tank at distances well over 1 000 metres. The Sd.Kfz.7 could carry gun crews of up to 12 men in theatre-type seats.

Available Now

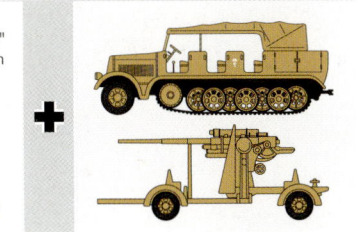

Panzer IV
Code: **A02308V**

1:76 RE-INTRODUCTION

Mould Tools made in 1971, pack illustration by Roy Cross, 1971. The Panzer IV was the most widely manufactured and deployed German tank of WWII. It was robust and reliable, seeing service in all combat theatres involving German forces. It was the only German tank to be in continuous production throughout the war with over 8,800 produced between 1936 and 1945.

Available Now

German Reconnaissance Set
Code: **A02312V**

1:76 RE-INTRODUCTION

The Sd kfz222 performed well enough in countries with good road networks, like those in Western Europe.

The Volkswagen Kübelwagen was a military vehicle designed by Ferdinand Porsche.

Available Sept-19

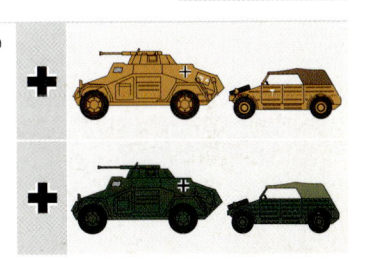

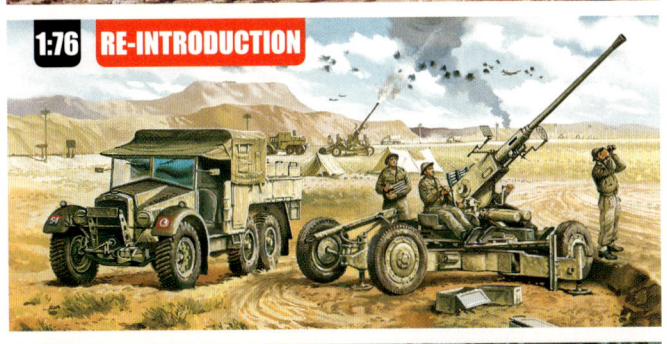

Bofors 40mm Gun & Tractor
Code: **A02314V**

1:76 RE-INTRODUCTION

Mould Tools made in 1976, pack illustration by Ken McDonough, 1976. Designed in 1930 by the Swedish Bofors Company, this gun was adopted by some 18 countries and became the standard light anti aircraft weapon with the British forces. The Morris CS8 15-cwt 4x2 General Service Trucks were made in large numbers and they became the backbone of the British Army.

Available Now

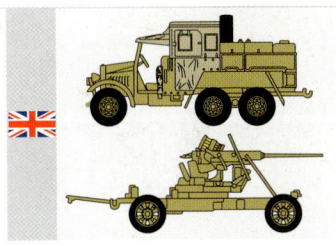

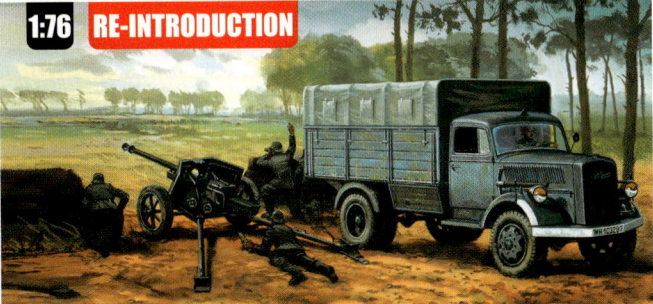

Pak 40 Gun & Truck
Code: **A02315V**

1:76 RE-INTRODUCTION

Mould Tools made in 1980, pack illustration by Ken McDonough, 1980. The PAK 40 formed the backbone of the German anti-tank gun forces throughout the latter part of the second world war. It was not as powerful as the famous 88mm gun, however, it was smaller and easier to conceal. The set is representative of a German anti-tank unit towards the end of the war.

Available Now

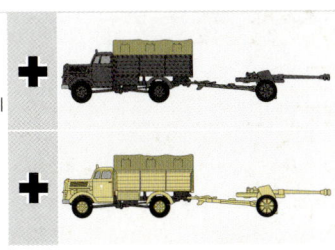

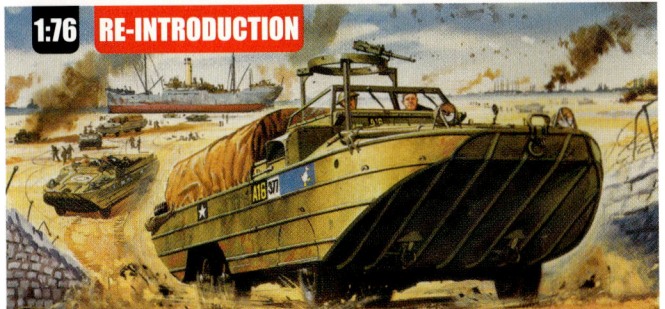

DUKW
Code: **A02316V**

1:76 RE-INTRODUCTION

The DUKW (popularly pronounced 'duck') is a six-wheel-drive amphibious truck that was designed for transporting goods and troops over land and water. The DUKW was used in landings in the Mediterranean, Pacific and on the D-Day beaches of Normandy.

Available May-19

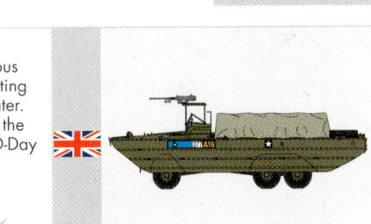

1:76 SCALE VINTAGE CLASSICS

www.airfix.com

1:76 SCALE VINTAGE CLASSICS

M3 Half-Track
Code: **A02318V**

Mould Tools made in 1966, pack illustration by Roy Cross, 1966. The M3 Personnel carrier was developed from the four-wheeled scout car. During WWII more than 41,000 vehicles were produced. This version came with the improved M49 machine gun ring mount over the right hand front seat. Between 1942 and 1943, all M3 Half-Tracks were continually upgraded.

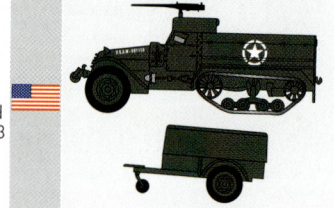

Available Feb-19

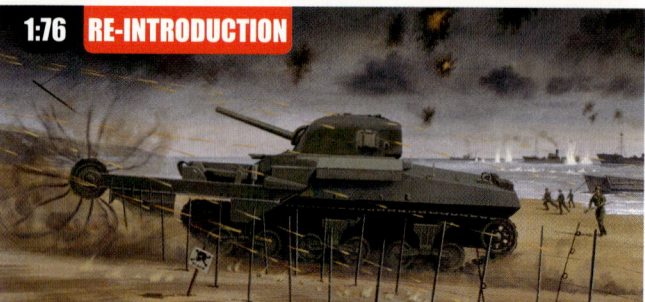

Sherman Crab
Code: **A02320V**

To support the infantry through the minefields on the ground operation in Europe and the Pacific, US military engineers decided to modify the Sherman, which was not only used by US forces, but also by the British, Canadian and Free French forces.

Available May-19

Churchill Crocodile
Code: **A02321V**

In 1943, British engineers developed the flame-thrower tank known as Crocodile, capable of producing a ten metre flame. These flames allowed the Allies to destroy bunkers and shelters without having to call the demolition teams of the infantry.

Available May-19

Sherman Calliope
Code: **A02334V**

The Rocket Launcher T34 (Calliope) was a tank-mounted multiple rocket launcher used by the US Army during WWII. The launcher was placed atop the tank, and fired a barrage of 4.5 in (114mm) rockets from 60 launch tubes. It adopts its name from the musical instrument 'Calliope', also known as the steam organ.

Available May-19

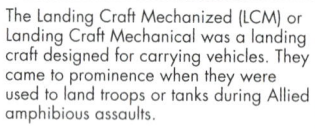

LCM3 & Sherman
Code: **A03301V**

The Landing Craft Mechanized (LCM) or Landing Craft Mechanical was a landing craft designed for carrying vehicles. They came to prominence when they were used to land troops or tanks during Allied amphibious assaults.

Available May-19

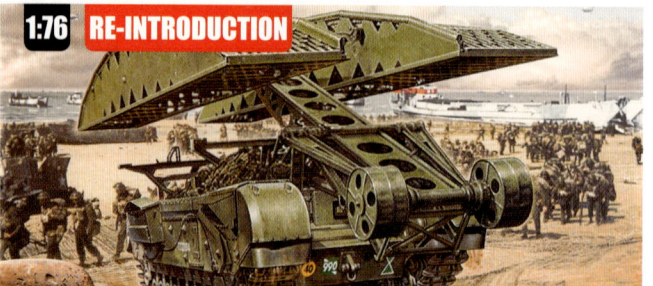

Churchill Bridge Layer
Code: **A04301V**

A variant of the Churchill tank, the bridge layer was created by the Royal Engineers and carried a 30ft long Small Box Girder (SBG) bridge. This proved invaluable for crossing many water filled obstacles as the Allies progressed across Western Europe after D-Day.

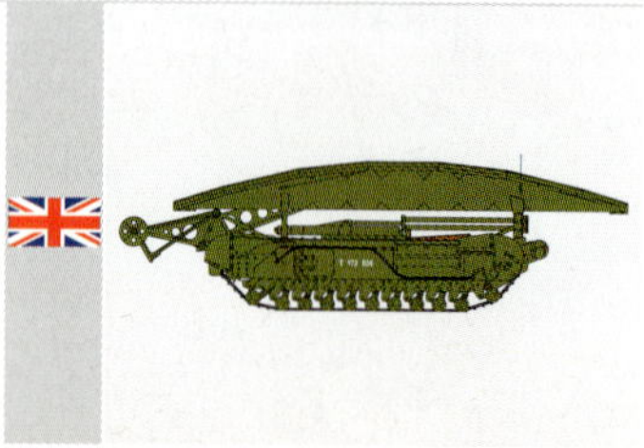

Available May-19

MILITARY FIGURES
WWII GERMAN INFANTRY

AIRFIX® VINTAGE CLASSICS

WWII German Infantry

1:76 RE-INTRODUCTION Code: A00705V

Mould Tools made in 1973, pack Illustration by William Stallion, 1973. Enjoy the nostalgia with Airfix Vintage Classics. In the early stages of WWII the standard German infantry uniform that was worn consisted of the field jacket, trousers tucked into black leather jackboots, and the characteristically shaped helmet. In the field, soldiers carried equipment including gas mask case, kit bag, shovel, canteen and ammunition pouch. This set of perfectly scaled figures and equipment includes an officer, grenade throwers and other key personnel from the Wehrmacht.

Available Jan-19

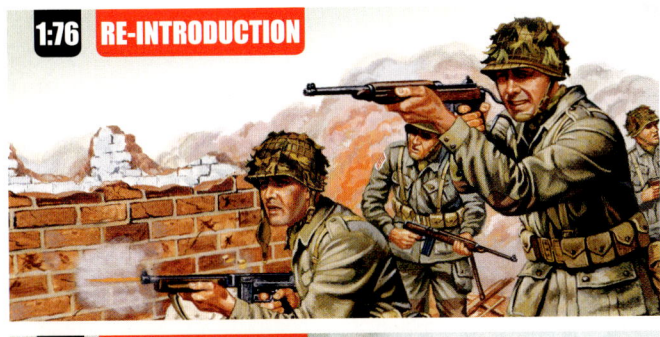

U.S. Paratroops

1:76 RE-INTRODUCTION Code: A00751V

Mould Tools made in 1975, pack Illustration by William Stallion, 1975. The American airborne landings in Normandy were the first United Sates combat operations of Operation Overlord. 13,100 paratroopers of the US 82nd Airborne and 101st Airborne Divisions made night parachute drops early on D-Day June 6th 1944.

Available Jan-19

WWII British Infantry

1:76 RE-INTRODUCTION Code: A00763V

Mould Tools made in 2011, pack Illustration by Brian Knight, 1973. Depicted here with an assortment of weapons, including the Bren Light Machine Gun and the Projector Infantry Anti-Tank (PIAT), these British Army Troops are as they would have appeared across occupied Europe, fighting to liberate France, Holland and Belgium.

Available Jan-19

1:76 SCALE VINTAGE CLASSICS

www.airfix.com

1:76 SCALE VINTAGE CLASSICS

8th Army
Code: **A00709V**

Mould Tools made in 1974, pack Illustration by Brian Knight, 1974. Commonly known as the "Desert Rats", the 8th Army figures are wearing their shorts and steel helmets in this 49 piece set. Included are mine detectors, machine gunners and riflemen.

Available Jan-19

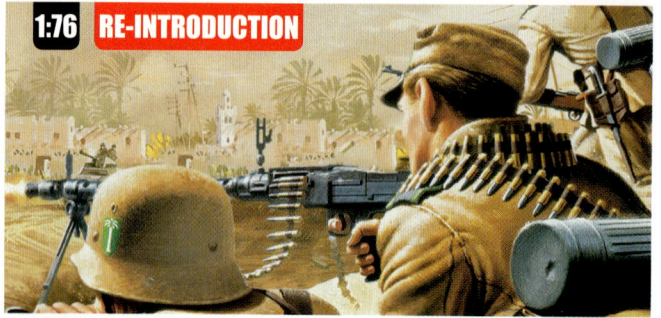

Afrika Korps
Code: **A00711V**

Mould Tools made in 1973, pack Illustration by William Stallion, 1973. Rommel's troops fought the 8th Army in the desert and the battles can be re-enacted with this superb set of figures, which includes a senior staff officer.

Available Jan-19

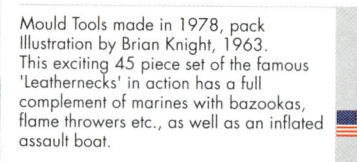

US Marines
Code: **A00716V**

Mould Tools made in 1978, pack Illustration by Brian Knight, 1963. This exciting 45 piece set of the famous 'Leathernecks' in action has a full complement of marines with bazookas, flame throwers etc., as well as an inflated assault boat.

Available Jan-19

RAF Personnel
Code: **A00747V**

Mould Tools made in 1972, pack Illustration by Brian Knight, 1972. The personnel included here are performing their various maintenance and rearming roles including some handling machine-guns, ammunition and even a camera.

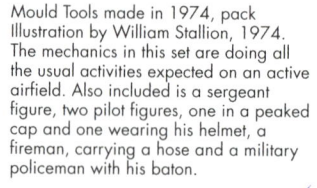

Available Feb-19

USAAF Personnel
Code: **A00748V**

Mould Tools made in 1974, pack Illustration by William Stallion, 1974. The mechanics in this set are doing all the usual activities expected on an active airfield. Also included is a sergeant figure, two pilot figures, one in a peaked cap and one wearing his helmet, a fireman, carrying a hose and a military policeman with his baton.

Available Feb-19

Luftwaffe Personnel
Code: **A00755V**

Mould Tools made in 1976, pack Illustration by William Stallion, 1976. At the beginning of WWII the Luftwaffe were by far the largest and most powerful airforce in the world. Figures in this set are posed loading, fixing and maintaining aircraft as well as having the inclusion of aircrew both standing and running.

Available Feb-19

Please visit www.airfix.com/catalogue2019 to locate your nearest Airfix stockist

WWI INFANTRY

AIRFIX VINTAGE CLASSICS

In vintage style packaging with classic illustrations, the WWI Airfix infantry figures make for fantastic diorama possibilities.

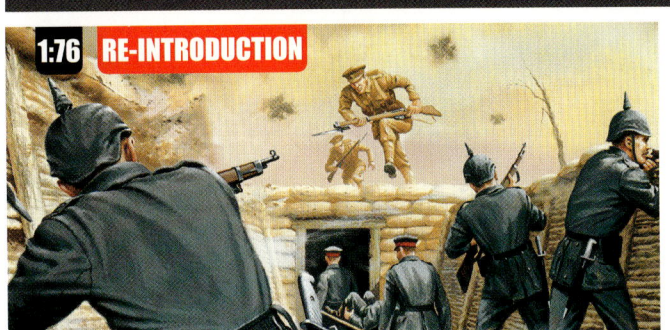

WWI German Infantry
Code: A00726V
1:76 RE-INTRODUCTION

Mould Tools made in 1966, pack Illustration by Brian Knight, 1970. Depicting the German Infantry at the beginning of the Great War this set includes a field officer, two infantry officers, a heavy machine gun with crew, and riflemen.

Available Now

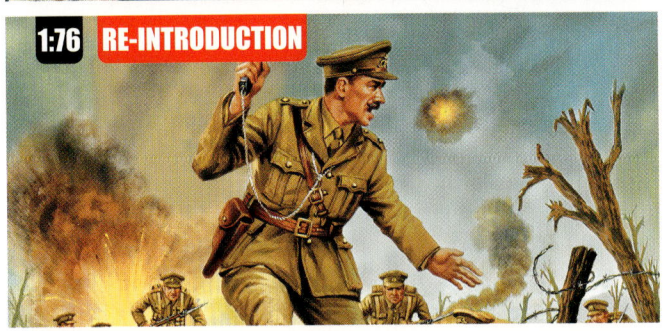

WWI British Infantry
Code: A00727V
1:76 RE-INTRODUCTION

Mould Tools made in 1966, pack Illustration by Brian Knight, 1970. The famous "Tommies" in this set are wearing the uniform of the early war period on the Western Front. Included are signallers, a wiring party and a trench mortar with crew.

Available Now

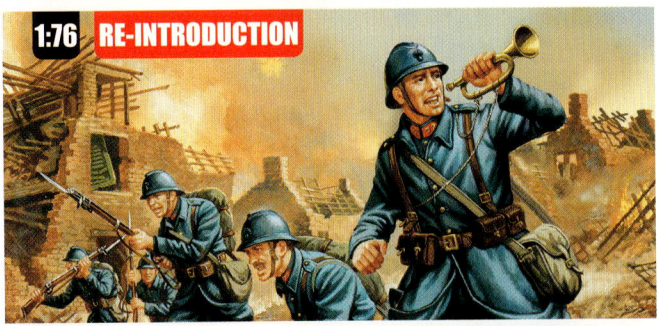

WWI French Infantry
Code: A00728V
1:76 RE-INTRODUCTION

Mould Tools made in 1966, pack Illustration by Brian Knight, 1970. The French Infantry took part in many of the largest and bloodiest battles of WWI whilst defending their homeland. The set features cyclists, a signaller complete with pigeons, a bugler, standard bearer and a variety of infantrymen.

Available Now

WWI U.S. Infantry
Code: A00729V
1:76 RE-INTRODUCTION

Mould Tools made in 1967, pack Illustration by Brian Knight, 1969. These are the "Doughboys" that arrived in France and took part in the last great battles of the First World War. Their equipment includes light machine guns and a remote-controlled rifle.

Available Now

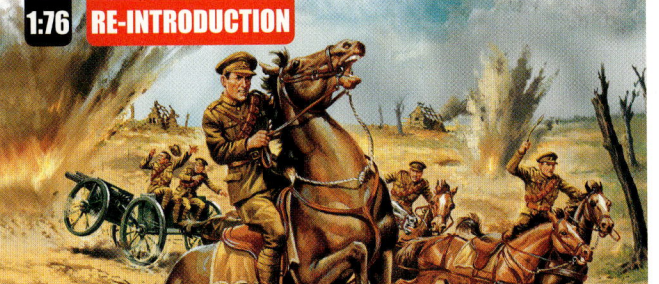

WWI Royal House Artillery
Code: A00731V
1:76 RE-INTRODUCTION

Mould Tools made in 1968, pack Illustration by Brian Knight, 1968. The Royal Horse Artillery was armed with light, mobile, horse-drawn guns. This set includes two field guns, a full team of horses, a gun limber and full crew.

Available Now

www.airfix.com

# AIRFIX SHIPS
VINTAGE CLASSICS

WASA Page 91

/ 1:72 / 1:130 / 1:144 / 1:180 / 1:600 SCALE VINTAGE CLASSICS

Please visit **www.airfix.com/catalogue2019** to locate your nearest Airfix stockist

1:600 RE-INTRODUCTION

HMS Victorious

Code: **A04201V**

HMS Victorious saw action in every theatre during WWII. From launching the aircraft that found the Bismarck, through to supporting the North African campaigns, working with the U.S. Navy in the Far East and famously taking a major part in the destruction of the Tirpitz. This model features the angled flight deck added in the 1950s

Available Sept-19

1:600 RE-INTRODUCTION

Admiral Graf Spee

Designed as a commerce raider on a displacement of only 10,000 ton, she became famous as a "Pocket Battleship." With heavier armour than her sister ships she was also the first German ship to be fitted with a form of radar. From September 1939 until December 1939 she raided allied shipping in the South Atlantic and Indian Ocean, sinking nine ships totaling 50,089 tons. She received extensive damage from HMS Ajax, Exeter and Achilles at the Battle of the River Plate and was scuttled by her Captain, Hans Langdorff, on December 17, 1939.

Available Sept-19 Code: **A04211V**

1:600 RE-INTRODUCTION

HMS Hood

Code: **A04202V**

Mould Tools made in 1960, pack illustration by Geoff Hunt, 1981. The largest warship in the world when launched in 1918. She was the pride of the Royal Navy on sailing to intercept the Bismarck in May 1941. After making contact with the German battleship she opened fire. The Bismarck returned fire and with her 5th salvo hit the Hood a fatal blow. She sank within two minutes.

Available Feb-19

1:600 SCALE VINTAGE CLASSICS

1:600 RE-INTRODUCTION

Bismarck

Available Feb-19   **Code: A04204V**

Mould Tools made in 1962, pack illustration by Geoff Hunt, 1979. The most powerful battleship in the world in 1941 when she sailed to raid Allied shipping in the North Atlantic with the heavy cruiser Prinz Eugen. After being spotted by the Royal Navy she was shadowed and then engaged. In this engagement the Bismarck sank HMS Hood. She was then damaged by at least one torpedo from attacking Swordfish, slowing her down. She was eventually sunk by torpedoes fired from Royal Naval ships with the loss of almost 1,900 crew.

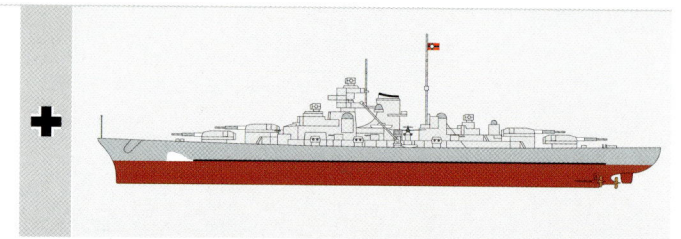

1:600 RE-INTRODUCTION

HMS Ark Royal

Available Feb-19   **Code: A04208V**

Mould Tools made in 1966, pack illustration by Roy Cross, 1966 The aircraft carrier Ark Royal was the third vessel of the Royal Navy to bear the name. She was launched at the Birkenhead shipyard of Cammel Laird on the 13th April 1937. H.M.S. Ark Royal was involved in the sinking of the German Battleship Bismarck but later, while on Malta convoy duty, was torpedoed by the German submarine U-81. Despite all attempts to tow her to Gibraltar, the Ark Royal slowly heeled over and at 0613 hrs. on 14th November 1941 she finally went down, only one sailor losing his life.

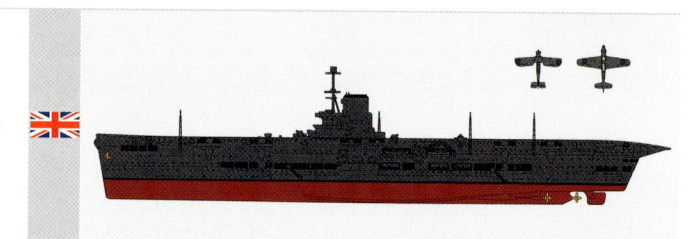

1:600 RE-INTRODUCTION

HMS *Belfast*

Available Feb-19   **Code: A04212V**

Mould Tools made in 1973, pack illustration by Roy Cross, 1973. During the Second World War HMS *Belfast* saw action at the Battle of North Cape in 1943 and played a major role during the D-Day landings in 1944. After a well-earned refit *Belfast* also played an active role in the Korean War from 1950-1952. One of only three surviving bombardment vessels from D-Day, HMS *Belfast* is now preserved by IWM and anchored in the River Thames near to Tower Bridge in London.

IWM records and tells the stories of those who have lived, fought and died in conflict since 1914. Your purchase ensures these stories are heard.
IWM.ORG.UK

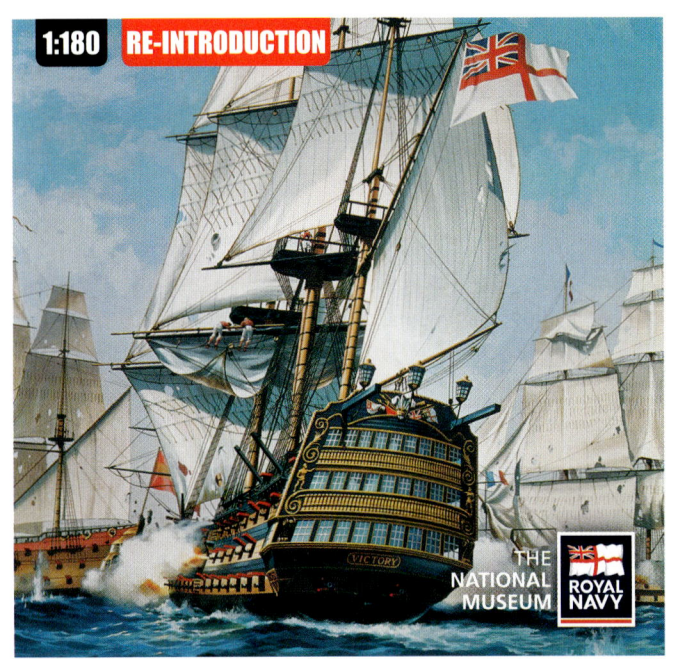

1:180 RE-INTRODUCTION

HMS Victory
Code: A09252V

Mould Tools made in 1965, pack illustration by Brian Knight, 1965. Launched an May 7th 1765, HMS Victory gained its fame by becoming Admiral Nelson's flagship during the Battle of Trafalgar in 1805. The victory at this battle ended Napolean's bid for mastery of the sea, but cost Admiral Nelson his life. She is now the oldest serving Royal Naval ship still in service.

Available Feb-19

1:130 RE-INTRODUCTION

Cutty Sark
Code: A09253V

Mould Tools made in 1967, pack illustration by Brian Knight, 1967. The Cutty Sark, built in Dumbarton, is the best known clipper and in her hey-day was the fastest of them all. She could carry 32000 square feet of sail giving her a maximum speed of over 17 knots. She was used to speed the new season's tea crop from China to London where the crews hoped to gain the prestige of being the first back.

Available Feb-19

1:144 RE-INTRODUCTION

WASA
Code: A09256V

In 1628 the Wasa disastrously keeled over and sank in Stockholm harbour at the start of it's maiden voyage. It was one of four ships built at the time to strengthen the Swedish Navy. She was raised in 1961, approximately 333 years later, and is now on display in a permanent restoration site in Stockholm.

Available Sept-19

1:72 RE-INTRODUCTION

Golden Hind
Code: A09258V

Mould Tools made in 1977, pack illustration by Geof Hunt ,1977.The Golden Hind was an English galleon best known for its global circumnavigation between 1577 and 1580, captained by Sir Francis Drake, who on his return with a haul of Spanish gold and other treasures was knighted by Queen Elizabeth.

Available Feb-19

1:72 / 1:30 / 1:144 / 1:180 SCALE VINTAGE CLASSICS

www.airfix.com

SPACE 50TH ANNIVERSARY 1969-2019

It's been 50 years since man first steped on the moon. Celebrate the history of space travel with these classic models from Airfix.

RE-INTRODUCED Apollo Saturn V

Apollo Saturn V

1:144 RE-INTRODUCTION Available May-19 — Code: **A11170**

The Saturn V, developed at NASA's Marshall Space Flight Center under the direction of Wernher von Braun, was the largest in a family of liquid-propellant rockets that solved the problem of getting to the Moon. The three stage rocket was taller than a 36-story building and was the largest, most powerful rocket ever built. A total of thirty-two Saturns of all types were launched; with not one failing. Thirteen of these were Vs. With a cluster of five powerful engines in each of the first two stages and using high-performance liquid hydrogen fuel for the upper stages, the Saturn V was one of the great feats of 20th-century engineering. Inside, the rocket contained three million parts in a labyrinth of fuel lines, pumps, gauges, sensors, circuits, and switches– each of which had to function reliably. The first manned Saturn V sent the Apollo 8 astronauts into orbit around the Moon in December 1968. After two more missions to test the Lunar Module, in July 1969 a Saturn V launched the crew of Apollo 11 to the first manned landing on the Moon.

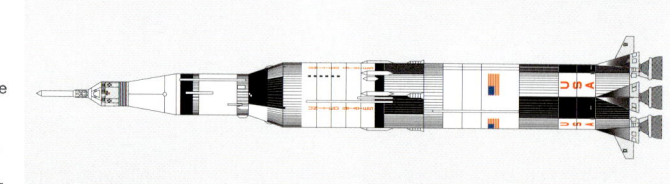

1:72 RE-INTRODUCTION

Gift Set Includes:
- Paints, brushes and glue
- Diorama base

One Step for Man... 50th Anniversary of 1st Manned Moon Landing

50 years ago, American Neil Armstrong became the first man to walk on the Moon. The astronaut stepped onto the Moon's surface, in the Sea of Tranquility, at 02:56 GMT, nearly 20 minutes after first opening the hatch on the Eagle landing craft. Armstrong had earlier reported the lunar module's safe landing at 20:17 GMT with the words: 'Houston, Tranquility Base here. The Eagle has landed.' As he put his left foot down first Armstrong declared: 'That's one small step for man, one giant leap for mankind.' He described the surface as being like powdered charcoal and the landing craft only left a small indentation on the surface.

Available May-19 — Code: **A50106**

Astronauts

Code: **A00741V**

This 57 part set consists of US Astronaut action figures and equipment to transport them across the surface of the moon. Includes two moon rovers and various other accessories.

Available May-19

Please visit www.airfix.com/catalogue2019 to locate your nearest Airfix stockist

RE-INTRODUCTION
RNLI SEVERN CLASS LIFEBOAT

Photo Credit: RNLI/Nicholas Leach

Lifeboats
A MINIMUM OF £1.25 FROM THE SALE OF THIS PRODUCT WILL BE PAID IN SUPPORT OF THE RNLI.

RNLI Severn Class Lifeboat

1:72 RE-INTRODUCTION

Available June-19 Code: **A07280**

The Severn class lifeboat is the largest lifeboat in the RNLI fleet introduced into the fleet in 1995. As an all-weather lifeboat, she can take on the worst sea conditions and comes into her own on long offshore searches and rescues. When lives are at risk out at sea, time is of the essence. With a top speed of 25 knots and a range of 250 nautical miles, the Severn class lifeboat can reach casualties fast in calm or rough seas. She carries a small powered Y boat, ideal for rescues near rocks and shallow waters, and can be launched using the Severn's integral crane. The kit in this box enables a fully detailed model of this RNLI Lifeboat to be built. Full detail of the outside deck, hull and fittings are included and by removing the cabin roof a fully detailed interior can be viewed. The decal scheme will allow any one of the current operational RNLI Severn Class lifeboats to be modelled.

*Payments are made to RNLI (Sales) Ltd (which pays all its taxable profits to the RNLI, a charity registered in England and Wales (209603) and Scotland (SC037736). Registered charity number 20003326 in the Republic of Ireland, of West Quay Road, Poole, Dorset BH15 1HZ

AIRFIX ENGINEER

Both these kits are available from many Airfix and Humbrol stockists and are a fabulous way to build and understand the two major types of engine used by today's modern world. Both come in kit form but with no gluing needed. All the major components work as they do in the real engine, so they're a great way to learn about how the real thing is constructed and works.

Internal Combustion Engine

With the sound of the start-up and the engine firing, this fantastic engine is a marvellous and fun way to learn about the Internal Combustion Engine. Over 100 pieces to put together makes all the details come alive.

Batteries required: 3 x AA

Available Now Code: **A42509**

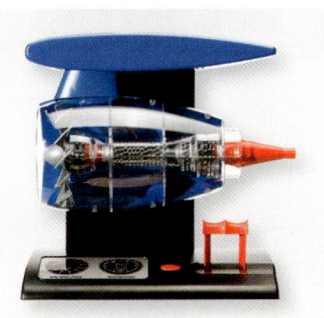

Jet Engine

With spinning turbo fans and a variable speed control, this is a brilliant way to understand the working features of the Jet Engine. Coming in 50 parts this working model is easily constructed into a really fun item.

Batteries required: 4 x 1.5v C

Available Now Code: **A20005**

LIFEBOAT & AIRFIX ENGINEER

www.airfix.com

BATTLES
AIRFIX BOARD GAME

A fast and fun introductory wargame playable with all your Airfix figures and vehicles. Airfix Battles comes with everything you need to play exciting World War II battles straight out of the box, including die-cut carboard counters for tanks, infantry and guns in case you don't have any figures to hand.

Battles - The Introductory Wargame

Code: **MUH050360**

Airfix Battles lets you plan your army using the Force Deck. Draw the cards or select the ones you need to build an exciting army to challenge your friends. Set up the battle using step-by-step instructions in the Mission Book and you're ready to play. Each player has a hand of Command Cards to move and fight their forces, bring in airstrikes or artillery support. You never know what your opponent is going to do next!

Contents:
- 2 x Double-sided A2 (420mm x 594mm) maps
- Over 100 carboard counters of tanks, infantry and terrain
- 1 x 16 Page Mission Book
- 1 x 24 Page Rule Book
- 1 x 54 Card Force Deck
- 1 x 54 Card Command Deck
- 10 x Six-side dice

Available Jan-19

Please visit www.airfix.com/catalogue2019 to locate your nearest Airfix stockist

TECHNICAL INDEX

The technical index on the following pages gives much more information about all the fantastic models in the Airfix range for 2019. This gives you the chance to compare sizes, number of pieces and the choices available.

KEY TO MILITARY ROUNDELS

Royal Flying Corps, Royal Air Force, Fleet Air Arm, Army Air Corps	Mongolian People's Air Force	Czech Air Force
Royal Air Force South East Asia Command	Imperial Japanese Army Air Force / Imperial Japanese Navy Air Service	Dutch Army / Dutch Air Force
Luftwaffe	Finnish Air Force	Slovakian Air Arm
Australian Air Force	Iranian Air Force	Indian Air Force
USAAF United States Army Air Force / USN United States Navy	French Air Force	Swedish Air Force
USAF United States Air Force / USN United States Navy	Aéronavale (French Navy Air Force)	Fuerza Aérea Dominicana
Royal New Zealand Air Force	People's Republic of Korea Air Force	South African Air Force
Italian Air Force	Hungarian Air Force	Danish Air Service
Belgian Air Force	The Irish Air Corps	Argentine Navy
Soviet Union Red Air Force	Chinese Air Force	Condor Legion
Yugoslavian Air Force	Polish Air Force	Romanian Air Force 1942/43
Italian Air Force 1939/43	Argentine Air Force	Bulgarian Air Force 1941/44
Spanish Air Force	Royal Canadian Air Force	Free French Air Force
Swiss Air Force	North Vietnamese Air Force	Norwegian Air Force

KEY TO FLAGS

Union Flag	New Zealand	Swedish Navy
Spain	Holland	United States
Italy	Canada	Soviet Union
Australia	White Ensign (Royal Navy)	Imperial Japan

www.airfix.com

TECHNICAL INDEX CONTINUED

Code	Model kit	Scale	Length	Width	Pieces	Options	Skill Level	Flying Hours	Page
QUICKBUILD									
J6017	VW Camper Van red		198	85	52	1	1	1	12
J6024	VW Camper Van blue		198	85	52	1	1	1	12
J6023	VW Beetle yellow		183	74	36	1	1	1	12
J6032	VW Camper 'Surfin'' NEW		198	85	52	1	1	1	13
J6031	Flower-Power VW Beetle NEW		183	74	36	1	1	1	13
J6019	Lamborghini Aventador white		199	94	33	1	1	1	14
J6020	Bugatti Veyron 16.4 black/red		187	89	34	1	1	1	14
J6021	McLaren P1™ green		193	90	36	1	1	1	14
J6045	D-Day Spitfire NEW		215	270	34	1	1	1	15
J6046	D-Day P-51D Mustang™ NEW		213	242	38	1	1	1	15
J6000	Spitfire		215	270	34	1	1	1	16
J6001	Messerschmitt Bf109		225	252	39	1	1	1	16
J6016	P-51D Mustang™		213	242	38	1	1	1	16
J6018	Red Arrows Hawk		221	180	31	1	1	1	17
J6003	BAE Hawk		221	180	31	1	1	1	17
J6002	Eurofighter Typhoon		231	160	30	1	1	1	18
J6005	F-22® Raptor®		208	152	27	1	1	1	18
J6009	Harrier		229	150	28	1	1	1	18
J6004	Apache™		252	189	40	1	1	1	19
J6010	Challenger Tank		216.7	75	35	1	1	1	19
J6022	Challenger Tank		217	75	35	1	1	1	19
STARTER & GIFT SETS									
A55114	Starter Set Mary Rose RE-INTRODUCTION	1:72	164	69	29	1	1	1	22
A55117	Willys MB Jeep® NEW	1:72	Various	Various	71	1	1	1	23
A55100	Supermarine Spitfire Mk.Ia - Small Starter Set	1:72	127	156	36	1	1	1	24
A55101	Curtiss Tomahawk IIb - Small Starter Set	1:72	135.5	158	47	1	1	1	24
A55104	HMS Victory - Small Starter Set	ftb	145	na	19	1	1	1	24
A55105	RAF Red Arrows Gnat - Small Starter Set	1:72	155	102	49	1	1	1	24
A55106	Messerschmitt B109E-3 - Small Starter Set	1:72	120	137	64	1	1	1	24

Code	Model kit	Scale	Length	Width	Pieces	Options	Skill Level	Flying Hours	Page
STARTER & GIFT SETS Continued									
A55116A	Hunting Percival Jet Provost T3 - Small Starter Set	1:72	137	156	45	1	1	1	25
A55107	North American Mustang IV™ - Small Starter Set	1:72	136	157	53	1	1	1	25
A55109	Cromwell MkIV Tank - Small Starter Set	1:76	88	39	91	1	2	1	25
A55110	Focke Wulf 190A-8 - Small Starter Set	1:72	125	145	53	1	1	1	25
A55111	Hawker Hurricane Mk.1 - Small Starter Set	1:72	133	171	51	1	1	1	25
A55210	Multipose WWII German Infantry Starter Set	1:32	n/a	n/a	102	n/a	1	1	25
A50089A	Aston Martin DB5 - Medium Start Set	1:32	143	52	47	1	1	1	26
A55200	Jaguar E Type - Medium Starter Set	1:32	136	52	49	1	1	1	26
A55201	Triumph Herald - Medium Starter Set	1:32	120	45	73	1	1	1	26
A55207	VW Beetle - Medium Starter Set	1:32	128	48	53	1	1	1	26
A55203	Douglas A-4B Skyhawk Multipose - Medium Starter Set	1:72	178	116	75	1	1	1	26
A55202C	RAF Red Arrows Hawk with RAF 100 scheme - Medium Starter Set	1:72	163	130	59	1	1	1	27
A55204	de Havilland Vampire T.11 - Medium Starter Set	1:72	146	161	55	1	1	1	27
A55205	Hawker Harrier GR.1 - Medium Starter Set	1:72	193	107	89	1	1	1	27
A55208	Hawker Typhoon Mk.Ib - Medium Starter Set	1:72	134	174	74	1	1	1	27
A55213	Boulton Paul Defiant Mk.I - Medium Starter Set	1:72	150	166	70	1	1	1	27
A55214	Grumman F4F-4 Wildcat - Medium Starter Set	1:72	120	159	58	1	1	1	27
A55301	Panavia Tornado F3 - Large Starter Set **RE-INTRODUCTION**	1:72	232	193	168	1	2	1	28
A55311	McDonnell Douglas F-15A Strike Eagle - Large Starter Set **NEW SCHEME RE-INTRODUCTION**	1:72	270	181	125	1	2	1	28
A55312	General Dynamics F-16A/B® Fighting Falcon® - Large Starter Set **NEW SCHEME RE-INTRODUCTION**	1:72	210	131	81	1	2	1	29
A55313	McDonnell Douglas F-18A Hornet - Large Starter Set **NEW SCHEME RE-INTRODUCTION**	1:72	237	172	94	1	2	1	29
A55303	King Tiger Tank - Medium Starter Set	1:76	135	49	89	1	2	1	30
A50098	Eurofighter Typhoon - Large Starter Set	1:72	221	152	65	1	3	2	30
A55300	BAE Harrier GR.9A - Large Starter Set	1:72	198	130	126	1	2	1	30
A55305	English Electric Lightning F.2A - Large Starter Set	1:72	235	148	92	1	2	1	30
A55307A	Westland Sea King HAR.3 - Large Starter Set	1:72	307	263	135	1	3	1	30
A50110	Aston Martin DBR9 - Large Starter Set	1:32	149	63	52	1	2	1	31

TECHNICAL INDEX CONTINUED

Code	Model kit	Scale	Length	Width	Pieces	Options	Skill Level	Flying Hours	Page
STARTER & GIFT SETS Continued									
A55302	Ford Fiesta WRC - Large Starter Set	1:32	125	60	79	1	2	1	31
A55304	MINI Coutryman WRC - Large Starter Set	1:32	127	58	71	1	2	1	31
A55306	Jaguar XKR GT3 - Large Starter Set	1:32	152	58	49	1	2	1	31
A55308	Ford 3 Litre GT - Large Starter Set	1:32	132	58	53	1	1	1	31
A55310	MINI Cooper S - Large starter set	1:32	118	59	73	1	1	1	31
A50181	RAF Centenary: Sopwith Camel / Spitfire Mk.Ia / Eurofighter Typhoon - Gift set	1:72	127/221	155/152	36/65	1	2		33
A50160	Supermarine Spitfire Mk Vb Messerschmitt Bf109E Dogfight Doubles Gift Set	1:48	194/183	234/205	90/107	1	3	3	33
A50097	Avro Vulcan B Mk2 XH558 Gift Set	1:72	446	469	108	1	3	4	33
A50162A	D-Day 75th Anniversary Operation Overlord - Gift Set RE-INTRODUCTION	1:76	600	340	410	1	2	5	34
A50009A	D-Day 75th Anniversary Battlefront Gift - Gift Set RE-INTRODUCTION	1:76	340	240	121	1	2	2	34
A50156A	D-Day 75th Anniversary Sea Assault - Gift Set RE-INTRODUCTION	1:76	340	240	179	1	2	3	35
A50157A	D-Day 75th Anniversay Air Assault - Gift Set RE-INTRODUCTION	1:76	340	240	189	1	2	3	35
A55314	RMS Titanic - Starter Set NEW	1:1000	275	29	74	1	2	1	37
A50164A	RMS Titanic - Gift Set RE-INTRODUCTION	1:700	385	43	141	1	2	3	36
A50146A	RMS Titanic - Gift Set RE-INTRODUCTION	1:400	670	-	381	1	4	4	37
MILITARY AIRCRAFT									
A01020A	Focke-Wulf Fw190A-8 NEW SCHEMES RE-INTRODUCTION	1:72	125	145	53	1	1	1	40
A01003	Curtiss Hawk 81-A-2 RE-INTRODUCTION	1:72	134.5	158	47	1	1	1	40
A01004A	North American P-51D Mustang™	1:72	136	157	53	1	1	1	41
A01005	Mitsubishi A6M2b Zero RE-INTRODUCTION	1:72	126	166	47	1	1	1	41
A01008A	Messerschmitt Bf109E-4	1:72	120	137	64	1	1	1	41
A01010	Hawker Hurricane Mk.I	1:72	133	171	51	1	1	1	41
A01071B	Supermarine Spitfire Mk.1a	1:72	127	155	36	1	1	1	41
A01087	Fokker E.III Eindecker	1:72	100	140	35	1	2	1	41
A02041A	Hawker Typhoon Mk.IB NEW SCHEMES	1:72	134	174	74	2	1	1	42
A02052A	Gloster Gladiator Mk.I/Mk.II NEW SCHEMES	1:72	118	137	51	2	2	1	42
A02058A	de Havilland Vampire T.11/J-28C	1:72	146	161	55	2	1	1	42
A02107	Hunting Percival Jet Provost T.4 NEW SCHEMES	1:72	137	156	45	2	1	1	43
A02029A	Messerschmitt Bf109G-6	1:72	125	137	41	2	1	1	43

Please visit www.airfix.com/catalogue2019 to locate your nearest Airfix stockist

Code	Model kit		Scale	Length	Width	Pieces	Options	Skill Level	Flying Hours	Page
MILITARY AIRCRAFT Continued										
A02069	Boulton Paul Defiant Mk.I		1:72	150	166	70	2	1	1	43
A02070	Grumman F4F-4 Wildcat		1:72	120	159	58	2	1	1	43
A02074	Grumman Martlet Mk.IV		1:72	120	160	54	2	2	1	43
A02101	Royal Aircraft Factory BE2c		1:72	115	156	54	2	2	1	44
A02102	Supermarine Spitfire Mk.VA		1:72	180	137	62	2	2	1	44
A02103	Hunting Percival Jet Provost T.3		1:72	137	156	45	2	1	1	44
A02104	Royal Aircraft Factory BE2C		1:72	115	156	54	2	2	1	44
A02105	Folland Gnat T.1		1:72	155	102	49	2	1	1	44
A02106	de Havilland Tiger Moth		1:72	102	124	42	2	2	1	44
A03029A	Douglas A4 Skyhawk	NEW SCHEMES RE-INTRODUCTION	1:72	178	116	75	2	2	1	45
A03080A	Messerschmitt Bf110C		1:72	169	226	100	2	2	1	45
A03085A	BAe Hawk T.Mk.1A		1:72	163	130	59	2	1	1	45
A03087	Junkers Ju87 B-1 Stuka		1:72	152	19	110	2	2	1	45
A03088	Messerschmitt Me262A-1a		1:72	148	174	65	2	2	1	45
A03090	Messerschmitt ME262A-2a	NEW SCHEMES NEW PARTS	1:72	148	174	65	2	2	1	46
A04016	Bristol Blenheim Mk.1	RE-INTRODUCTION	1:72	168	237	142	2	2	2	47
A04062	Messerschmitt Me262B-1a/V1		1:72	152	192	74	3	2	1	47
A03091	Mikoyan-Gurevich MiG-17F Fresco	NEW MOULD	1:72	156	134	87	2	2	1	48-49
A04003	Supermarine Swift F.R. Mk5		1:72	180	137	62	2	2	1	50
A04019	Bristol Beaufighter Mk.X		1:72	175	246	120	2	2	2	50
A04053A	Fairey Swordfish Mk.1		1:72	154	193	125	2	3	2	50
A04056	Westland Sea King HC.4		1:72	307	263	133	2	2	2	50
A04058	Nakajima B5N2 'Kate'		1:72	142	214	107	2	2	2	50
A04059	Bristol Blenheim Mk.If		1:72	168	237	142	2	2	2	50
A05330	RAF Bomber Re-Supply Set		1:72	n/a	n/a	197	1	2	2	51
A06304	USAAF Eighth Air Force Bomber Re-supply Set		1:72	n/a	n/a	200	1	2	2	51
A12010	Eighth Air Force Boeing B-17G™ and Bomber Re-Supply Set		1:72	320	438	449	1	3	4	51
A04060	Nakajima B5N1 'Kate'		1:72	142	214	107	2	2	2	52
A04063	Westland Sea King HAS.3		1:72	307	263	133	2	2	2	52

TECHNICAL INDEX CONTINUED

Code	Model kit		Scale	Length	Width	Pieces	Options	Skill Level	Flying Hours	Page
MILITARY AIRCRAFT Continued										
A05042A	English Electric Lightning F6		1:72	234	148	132	2	2	2	52
A05043	Bristol Beaufighter TF.10		1:72	175	246	120	2	2	2	52
A06015	North American B25C/D Mitchell™		1:72	233	286	165	2	3	3	52
A06019	McDonnell Douglas FG.1 Phantom - RAF	NEW SCHEMES	1:72	247	162	161	2	3	3	53
A06017	McDonnell Douglas FGR2 Phantom	NEW SCHEMES NEW PARTS	1:72	247	162	161	2	3	3	53
A06016	McDonnell Douglas FG.1 Phantom - RN		1:72	247	162	161	3	3	3	53
A06021	Blackburn Buccaneer S Mk.2 RN	NEW MOULD	1:72	268	186	141	3	3	3	54-55
A06020	North American B25B™ Mitchell 'Doolittle Raid'	NEW SCHEMES NEW PARTS	1:72	233	286	166	2	3	3	56
A07007	Heinkel He.111H-6		1:72	226	312	180	3	3	2	56
A08013A	Avro Lancaster B.III		1:72	294	432	235	2	3	3	56
A08015A	Douglas Dakota Mk.IIII™		1:72	273	400	145	2	3	3	56
A08020	Vickers Wellington Mk.VIII	NEW SCHEMES NEW PARTS	1:72	273	364	177	2	3	3	57
A08019	Vickers Wellington Mk.IC		1:72	273	364	133	2	3	3	57
A08017	Boeing B17G Flying Fortress™		1:72	320	438	245	2	3	3	58
A08017A	Boeing B17G Flying Fortress™	NEW SCHEMES	1:72	320	438	245	4	3	3	58
A08016	Armstrong Whitworth Whitley Mk.V		1:72	312	356	155	2	3	3	58
A08018	Boeing Fortress Mk.III™		1:72	320	438	245	2	3	3	58
A09007	Avro Lancaster B.III (Special) - The Dambusters		1:72	294	432	265	2	3	3	58
A09008	Douglas Dakota MkIII With Willys Jeep®		1:72	273	400	216	1	3	3	59
A09009	Armstrong Whitworth Whitley Mk.VII		1:72	312	356	155	2	3	3	59
A11004	Avro Shackleton MR2		1:72	388	508	279	2	3	4	59
A11005	Avro Shackleton AEW.2		1:72	370	508	242	2	3	4	59
A12008	Handley Page Victor B.Mk.2 (BS)		1:72	486	508	228	2	3	4	59
A12009	Handley Page Victor K.2/SR.2		1:72	486	508	228	3	3	4	59
A04104	de Havilland D.H.82a Tiger Moth	NEW MOULD	1:48	152	184	91	2	3	2	60
A05135	Supermarine Spitfire FR Mk.XIV	NEW MOULD	1:48	195	207	118	2	3	2	61
A05138	North American P51-D Mustang™	NEW SCHEMES NEW PARTS	1:48	205	236	147	2	3	3	62
A05129	Hawker Hurricane Mk.1 - Tropical		1:48	200	225	127	2	2	2	62
A05130	Curtiss P-40B Warhawk		1:48	202	237	106	2	2	2	62
A05132	Boulton Paul Defiant NF.1		1:48	185	238	158	2	2	2	62

Please visit www.airfix.com/catalogue2019 to locate your nearest Airfix stockist

Code	Model kit	Scale	Length	Width	Pieces	Options	Skill Level	Flying Hours	Page
MILITARY AIRCRAFT Continued									
A05136	North American F-51D Mustang™	1:48	205	236	145	3	3	3	62
A05137	North American Mustang Mk.IV™	1:48	205	236	147	2	3	3	63
A05120B	Messerschmitt Bf109E-3/E-4	1:48	183	205	107	3	3	2	63
A05133	Curtiss Tomahawk Mk.IIB	1:48	202	237	106	2	2	2	63
A05134	Hawker Sea Hurricane Mk.IB	1:48	200	255	127	2	2	2	63
A06106	Hawker Sea Fury FB.11 'Export'	1:48	231	244	122	3	2	2	64
A06101A	Supermarine Spitfire F.Mk.22/24	1:48	217	234	78	2	3	3	64
A07114A	Junkers Ju87 B-1 Stuka NEW SCHEME	1:48	229	288	158	3	3	3	64
A07115	Junkers Ju87B-2/R-2	1:48	229	288	159	2	3	3	64
A09179	English Electric Lightning F1/F1A/F3	1:48	350	220	153	3	3	3	64
A09189	Hawker Hunter F4 NEW SCHEMES NEW PARTS	1:48	291	214	124	3	3	3	65
A09185	Hawker Hunter F.6 NEW MOULD	1:48	280	210	116	3	3	3	65
A09186	Bristol Blenheim Mk.IF NEW MOULD	1:48	180	238	216	2	3	3	65
A09182	Gloster Meteor F.8	1:48	287	236	165	2	3	3	66
A09188	Gloster Meteor FR.9	1:48	287	236	165	2	3	3	66
A09184	Gloster Meteor F.8 (Korean War)	1:48	287	236	165	3	3	3	66
A09187	Supermarine Walrus Mk.1 'Silver Wings'	1:48	238	292	156	3	3	3	66
A10101A	English Electric Canberra B(i).6/B.20	1:48	416	406	182	2	3	4	66
A11002	de Havilland Sea Vixen RE-INTRODUCTION	1:48	340	317	227	4	4	4	66
A19003	Hawker Typhoon Mk.1B - Car Door	1:24	404	528	520	4	4	6	67
A19003A	Hawker Typhoon Mk.1B - Car Door (including additional German scheme) NEW SCHEME	1:24	404	528	520	5	4	6	67
A19004	Grumman F6F-5 Hellcat NEW MOULD	1:24	424	543	572	4	4	6	68-69
MILITARY VEHICLES AND DIORAMA SETS									
A02338	Cromwell Mk.IV Cruiser Tank	1:76	51	27	35	1	1	1	70
A02339	British Airborne Willys Jeep®	1:76	47	22	39	1	2	1	70
A02340	Higgins LCVP RE-INTRODUCTION	1:72	145	22	47	1	2	1	70
A03306	Bedford QLD/QLT Trucks RE-INTRODUCTION	1:76	90/79	32/32	74/61	2	2	1	70
A06361	17 Pdr Anti-Tank Gun	1:32	233	69	171	1	2	2	70
A1351	Panzer IV Ausf.H, Mid Version NEW	1:35	201	82	TBC	2	3	3	71

TECHNICAL INDEX CONTINUED

Code	Model kit		Scale	Length	Width	Pieces	Options	Skill Level	Flying Hours	Page
MILITARY VEHICLES AND DIORAMA SETS Continued										
A1352	Panther Ausf.G	NEW	1:35	247	98	TBC	2	3	3	71
A1353	JagdPanzer 38 tonne Hetzer, Late Version	NEW	1:35	243	91	TBC	2	3	3	71
A1354	Tiger-1, Early Version - Operation Citadel	NEW	1:35	241	102	TBC	2	4	3	71
A1355	JagdPanzer 38 tonne Hetzer, Early Version	NEW	1:35	243	91	TBC	2	3	3	71
A1356	M36B1 GMC (U.S. Army)	NEW	1:35	213	87	TBC	2	3	3	72
A1357	Tiger 1, Early Production Version	NEW	1:35	241	102	TBC	2	3	3	72
A1358	M3 Stuart, Honey (British Version)	NEW	1:35	TBC	TBC	TBC	2	3	3	72
A1359	Tiger-1, Mid Version	NEW	1:35	241	102	TBC	2	3	3	72
A1360	M10 GMC (U.S. Army)	NEW	1:35	195	87	TBC	2	3	3	72
A1361	T34/85, 112 Factory Production	NEW	1:35	191	86	TBC	2	3	3	72
A1362	German Light Tank Pz.Kpfw.35(t)	NEW	1:35	140	59	TBC	2	3	3	73
A1363	Tiger-1, Early Version	NEW	1:35	241	102	TBC	2	4	3	73
A1364	Tiger-1, Late Version	NEW	1:35	241	102	TBC	2	3	3	73
A1365	M4A3(76)W, Battle of the Bulge	NEW	1:35	171	80	TBC	2	3	3	73
A1366	M36/M36B2, Battle of the Bulge	NEW	1:35	213	87	TBC	2	3	3	73
A1367	U.S. Tractor	NEW	1:35	260	74	70	1	2	2	73
RUINED RESIN BUILDINGS										
A75010	Afghan Single Storey House		1:48	200	185	1	1	1	1	74
A75012	Narrow Road Bridge Broken Span		1:72	320	125	1	1	1	1	75
A75013	Italian Farmhouse		1:76	123	80	1	1	1	1	75
A75014	Italian Townhouse		1:76	70	106	1	1	1	1	75
A75015	Polish Bank		1:72	230	140	1	1	1	1	75
A75016	Czech Restaurant		1:72	130	80	1	1	1	1	75
A75017	European City Steps		1:72	155	40	1	1	1	1	75
VINTAGE CLASSICS AIRCRAFT										
A01047V	Fiesler Storch	RE-INTRODUCTION	1:72	138	199	52	1	2	1	76
A01052V	Hawker Demon	RE-INTRODUCTION	1:72	125	158	31	1	2	1	77
A01055V	Bristol Bulldog	RE-INTRODUCTION	1:72	50	53	48	1	2	1	77
A02051V	Henschel Hs123A-1	RE-INTRODUCTION	1:72	116	146	38	2	2	1	77

Code	Model kit		Scale	Length	Width	Pieces	Options	Skill Level	Flying Hours	Page
VINTAGE CLASSICS AIRCRAFT Continued										
A03001V	de Havilland Heron MkII	RE-INTRODUCTION	1:72	205	303	67	2	2	1	78
A03009V	Hawker Siddeley Dominie T.1	RE-INTRODUCTION	1:72	214	199	66	2	2	1	78
A03012V	Handley Page Jetstream	RE-INTRODUCTION	1:72	200	220	94	2	2	1	78
A04006V	Northrop P-61 Black Widow	RE-INTRODUCTION	1:72	210	279	112	2	2	2	78
A04007V	Savoia-Marchetti SM79	RE-INTRODUCTION	1:72	229	33	102	2	2	2	78
A05170V	Concorde Prototype BOAC	RE-INTRODUCTION	1:144	431	181	52	1	2	2	78
VINTAGE CLASSICS MILITARY VEHICLES										
A02335V	Matilda Hedgehog Tank	RE-INTRODUCTION	1:76	81	34	72	1	2	1	79
A02337V	WWI Female Tank	RE-INTRODUCTION	1:76	102	220	69	1	1	1	80
A01315V	WWI Male Tank Mk.I	RE-INTRODUCTION	1:76	102	22	49	1	2	1	80
A01316V	Russian T34	RE-INTRODUCTION	1:76	76	33	58	1	2	1	80
VINTAGE CLASSICS D DAY TANKS										
A01303V	Sherman M4 Mk1	RE-INTRODUCTION	1:76	75	35	55	1	2	1	81
A01302V	Panther	RE-INTRODUCTION	1:76	77	38	97	1	2	1	81
A01304V	Churchill Mk.VII	RE-INTRODUCTION	1:76	94	28	104	1	2	1	81
A01305V	25pdr Field Gun	RE-INTRODUCTION	1:76	161	n/a	71	1	2	1	81
A01306V	Stug III 75mm Assault Gun	RE-INTRODUCTION	1:76	71	39	79	1	2	1	81
A01308V	Tiger 1	RE-INTRODUCTION	1:76	82	49	68	1	2	1	82
A01309V	Bren Gun Carrier & 6 pdr AT Gun	RE-INTRODUCTION	1:76	121	27	45	1	2	1	82
A01311V	SDKFZ Armoured Car	RE-INTRODUCTION	1:76	76	26	57	1	2	1	82
A01314V	AEC Matador & 5.5inch Gun	RE-INTRODUCTION	1:76	184	31	67	1	2	1	82
A02301V	Scammell Tank Transporter	RE-INTRODUCTION	1:76	210	38	107	1	2	1	82
A02302V	Buffalo Amphibian LVT & Jeep®	RE-INTRODUCTION	1:76	101	44	107	1	2	1	82
A02303V	88mm Gun & Tractor	RE-INTRODUCTION	1:76	180	31	114	1	2	1	83
A02308V	Panzer IV	RE-INTRODUCTION	1:76	78	38	101	1	2	1	83
A02312V	German Reconnaisance Set	RE-INTRODUCTION	1:76	65/48	29/21	57	1	2	1	83
A02314V	Bofors Gun & Tractor	RE-INTRODUCTION	1:76	152	27	107	1	2	1	83
A02315V	Pak 40 Gun & Truck	RE-INTRODUCTION	1:76	155	28	65	2	2	1	83
A02316V	DUKW	RE-INTRODUCTION	1:76	125	33	50	1	1	1	83

TECHNICAL INDEX CONTINUED

Code	Model kit		Scale	Length	Width	Pieces	Options	Skill Level	Flying Hours	Page
VINTAGE CLASSICS D DAY TANKS Continued										
A02318V	Half-Track M3	RE-INTRODUCTION	1:76	131	36	54	1	2	1	84
A02320V	Sherman Crab	RE-INTRODUCTION	1:76	120	51	72	1	2	1	84
A02321V	Churchill Crocodile	RE-INTRODUCTION	1:76	155	38	128	1	2	1	84
A02334V	Sherman Calliope	RE-INTRODUCTION	1:76	75	33	74	1	2	1	84
A03301V	LCM3 & Sherman Tank	RE-INTRODUCTION	1:76	194/55	53/75	53/35	1	2	1	84
A04301V	Churchill Bridge Layer	RE-INTRODUCTION	1:76	150	49	129	1	2	2	84
VINTAGE CLASSICS MILITARY FIGURES										
A00705V	WWII German Infantry	RE-INTRODUCTION	1:76	n/a	n/a	48	n/a	1	1	85
A00751V	US Paratroops	RE-INTRODUCTION	1:76	n/a	n/a	48	n/a	1	1	85
A00763V	WWII British Infantry	RE-INTRODUCTION	1:76	n/a	n/a	48	n/a	1	1	85
A00709V	8th Army	RE-INTRODUCTION	1:76	n/a	n/a	49	n/a	1	1	86
A00711V	Afrika Korps	RE-INTRODUCTION	1:76	n/a	n/a	48	n/a	1	1	86
A00716V	US Marines	RE-INTRODUCTION	1:76	n/a	n/a	45	n/a	1	1	86
A00747V	RAF Personnel	RE-INTRODUCTION	1:76	n/a	n/a	48	n/a	1	1	86
A00748V	USAAF Personnel	RE-INTRODUCTION	1:76	n/a	n/a	46	n/a	1	1	86
A00755V	Luftwaffe Personnel	RE-INTRODUCTION	1:76	n/a	n/a	46	n/a	1	1	86
A00726V	WWI German Infantry	RE-INTRODUCTION	1:76	n/a	n/a	48	n/a	n/a	1	87
A00727V	WWI British Infantry	RE-INTRODUCTION	1:76	n/a	n/a	48	n/a	n/a	1	87
A00728V	WWI French Infantry	RE-INTRODUCTION	1:76	n/a	n/a	48	n/a	n/a	1	87
A00729V	WWI U.S. Infantry	RE-INTRODUCTION	1:76	n/a	n/a	48	n/a	n/a	1	87
A00731V	WWI Royal House Artillery	RE-INTRODUCTION	1:76	n/a	n/a	48	n/a	n/a	1	87
VINTAGE CLASSICS SHIPS										
A04201V	HMS Victorious	RE-INTRODUCTION	1:600	397	53	94	1	3	2	89
A04211V	Admiral Graf Spee	RE-INTRODUCTION	1:600	310	36	124	1	3	2	89
A04202V	HMS Hood	RE-INTRODUCTION	1:600	430	53	131	1	2	2	89
A04204V	Bismarck	RE-INTRODUCTION	1:600	415	60	170	2	3	2	90
A04208V	HMS Ark Royal	RE-INTRODUCTION	1:600	383	88	353	1	3	3	90
A04212V	HMS Belfast	RE-INTRODUCTION	1:600	311	35	250	1	3	2	90
A09252V	HMS Victory	RE-INTRODUCTION	1:180	383	88	353	1	3	4	91

Please visit www.airfix.com/catalogue2019 to locate your nearest Airfix stockist

Code	Model kit		Scale	Length	Width	Pieces	Options	Skill Level	Flying Hours	Page
VINTAGE CLASSICS SHIPS Continued										
A09253V	Cutty Sark	RE-INTRODUCTION	1:130	520	220	220	1	4	4	91
A09256V	WASA	RE-INTRODUCTION	1:144	486	229	229	1	4	4	91
A09258V	Golden Hind	RE-INTRODUCTION	1:72	360	87	109	1	3	3	91
SPACE										
A11170	Apollo Saturn V 50th Anniversary of 1st Manned Moon Landing	RE-INTRODUCTION	1:144	768	132	78	1	3	4	92
A50106	One Step for Man 50th Anniversary of 1st Manned Moon Landing	RE-INTRODUCTION	1:72	348	247	92/16	1	2	2	32 & 92
A00741V	Astronauts	RE-INTRODUCTION	1:76	n/a	n/a	59	n/a	1	1	92
RNLI SEVERN CLASS LIFEBOAT										
A07280	RNLI Severn Class Lifeboat	RE-INTRODUCTION	1:72	236	78	189	1	3	3	93
ENGINEER										
A42509	Combustion Engine		n/a	220	240	100	n/a	2	3	93
A20005	Jet Engine		n/a	200	380	50	n/a	2	3	93
BOARD GAME										
MUH050360	Battles	NEW	n/a	594	420	100+	n/a	n/a	n/a	94

Produced under licensed. Boeing, Douglas, McDonnell Douglas, A-4 Skyhawk, AH-64 Apache Longbow, B-17 Flying Fortress, B-25 Mitchell, C-47, DC-3, F-4 Phantom, P-51 Mustang their distinctive logos, product markings, and trade dress are all trademarks of The Boeing Company.

The Hawk family of aircraft are designed and manufactured by BAE Systems. BAE SYSTEMS is a registered trade mark of BAE Systems plc.

The RAF Red Arrows name and logo are trademarks of the UK Secretary of State for Defence and used under license.

The RAF name and logo are trademarks of the UK Secretary of State for Defence and used under licence.

"Aston Martin", "Aston Martin Racing" and related logos and other trademarks are owned, licensed and/or used by Aston Martin and Aston Martin Racing. These trademarks may not be used, amended and/or reproduced without permission. All rights are reserved.

The Gulf logo is a trademark/intellectual property right owned by and licensed from the Gulf Oil International Group and Gulf Oil Limited Partnership. The Gulf racing livery is a trademark/intellectual property right owned by and licensed from the Gulf Oil International Group.

The MINI Logo and the MINI wordmark are trademarks of BMW AG and are used under license.

Ford Motor Company Trademarks and Trade Dress used under license to Hornby Hobbies. Manufactured by Hornby Hobbies LTD.

Jaguar and the leaper device are trademarks owned and licensed by Jaguar Land Rover Limited.

The Triumph logo and the Triumph wordmark are trademarks of BMW AG and are used under License.

Trademarks, design patents and copyrights are used with the approval of the owner Volkswagen AG.

The Westland Sea King is a product of Leonardo MW Ltd and all rights in it, including its name, are hereby reserved. The models have been produced with the permission and assistance of Leonardo MW Ltd.

Standard is a trademark owned and licensed by British Motor Heritage Limited. Licensing agents LMI. www.bmh-ltd.com

Manufactured under license from McLaren Automotive Limited. The McLaren name and logo are registered trademarks of McLaren.

Vauxhall Motors Limited trademarks used under license to Hornby Hobbies Ltd.

Adam Opel AG Trademarks used under license to Hornby Hobbies

The trademarks copyrights and design rights in and associated with Lamborghini, Lamborghini with Bull and Shield Device, are used under license from Automobili Lamborghini S.p.A., Italy.

Trademarks design patents and copyrights are used with the approval of the owner and/or exclusive licensee Bugatti International SA.

Royal Naval Museum Trading Company Ltd - HMS Victory® is a registered trade mark and is used under licence by Hornby Hobbies Ltd" Profits from the sale of this product go towards the preservation of Naval heritage

Imperial War Museum Sales of this product support the work of the Imperial War Museum© Imperial War Museum/2018

Vulcan to the Sky Trust Made by Hornby Hobbies Ltd under license from Vulcan to the Sky Trust "Vulcan to the Sky Trust" and "XH558" are registered trademarks of Vulcan to the Sky Trust

Grumman Martlet Mk.IV™ and Grumman F4F-4 Wildcat™ are trademarks of Northrop Grumman Systems Corporation.

Copyright Mary Rose Trust

RNLI name and logo are trademarks of RNLI used by Hornby Hobbies Ltd under licence from RNLI (Sales) Ltd.

Jeep, the Jeep grille and related logos, vehicle model names and trade dress are trademarks of FCA US LLC and used under license by Hornby Hobbies LTD. ©2019 FCA US LLC.

GM General Motors Trademarks used under license to Hornby Hobbies Ltd.

LOCKHEED MARTIN, F-22® Raptor®, associated emblems and logos, and body designs of vehicles are either registered trademarks or trademarks of Lockheed Martin Corporation in the USA and/or other jurisdictions, used under license by Hornby Hobbies Ltd.

Where appropriate some of the content within this publication has been submitted for approval to Licensors / brand owners ahead of the products being developed. The images and content of the products may vary on production further to the Licensor's / brand owners comments. Every effort is made to give a true and fair representation of our products within this publication and we thank our partners for their support

Turn your model kit into a masterpiece using...

Humbrol™
Paints, Accessories & Craft Kits

Your guide to the full 2019 Humbrol range of paints and accessories starts here!

Humbrol
100 YEARS
1919 – 2019

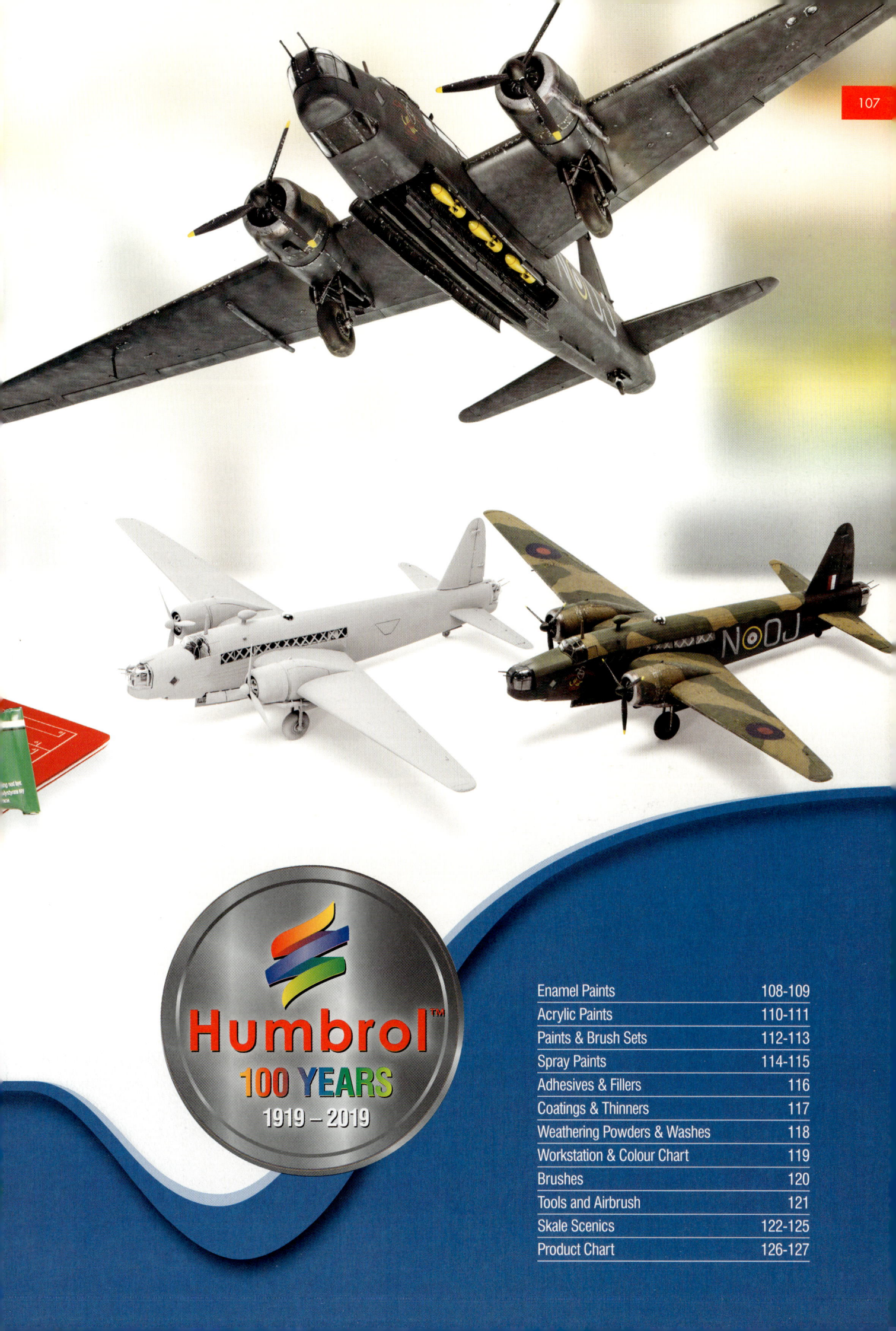

Enamel Paints	108-109
Acrylic Paints	110-111
Paints & Brush Sets	112-113
Spray Paints	114-115
Adhesives & Fillers	116
Coatings & Thinners	117
Weathering Powders & Washes	118
Workstation & Colour Chart	119
Brushes	120
Tools and Airbrush	121
Skale Scenics	122-125
Product Chart	126-127

100 YEARS OF Humbrol™ Enamel Paints

Matt Colours 14ml

No.	Code	Name
1	AA0014	Grey Primer
23	AA0254	Duck Egg Blue
24	AA0268	Trainer Yellow
25	AA0271	Blue
26	AA0285	Khaki
27	AA0299	Sea Grey
28	AA1496	Camouflage Grey
29	AA0312	Dark Earth
30	AA0326	Dark Green
31	AA0343	Slate Grey
32	AA1506	Dark Grey
33	AA0360 14ml / AQ0366 50ml	Black*
34	AA0374 14ml / AQ0383 50ml	White*
36	AA0036	Pastel Green
37	AA0037	Bright Green
42	AA0042	Violet
44	AA0044	Pastel Blue
46	AA0046	Orange
49	AA0535	Varnish
57	AA0057	Pastel Pink
58	AA0058	Magenta
60	AA0655	Scarlet
61	AA0669	Flesh
62	AA0672	Leather
63	AA0686	Sand
64	AA0713	Light Grey
65	AA0727	Aircraft Blue
66	AA0730	Olive Drab
67	AA0744	Tank Grey
70	AA0775	Brick Red
72	AA0792	Khaki Drill
73	AA0802	Wine
74	AA0816	Linen
75	AA0833	Bronze Green
76	AA0847	Uniform Green
77	AA0850	Navy Blue
78	AA0864	Cockpit Green
79	AA0878	Blue Grey
80	AA0881	Grass Green
81	AA0895	Pale Yellow
82	AA0905	Orange Lining
83	AA0919	Ochre
84	AA0922	Mid Stone
86	AA0953	Light Olive
87	AA0967	Steel Grey
88	AA0970	Deck Green
89	AA0984	Middle Blue
90	AA0998	Beige Green
91	AA1002	Black Green
93	AA1033	Desert Yellow
94	AA1047	Brown Yellow
96	AA1064	RAF Blue
98	AA1081	Chocolate
99	AA1095	Lemon
100	AA1105	Red Brown
101	AA1119	Mid Green
102	AA1122	Army Green
103	AA1136	Cream
104	AA1153	Oxford Blue
105	AA1167	Marine Green
106	AA1170	Ocean Grey
109	AA1208	WWI Blue
110	AA1211	Natural Wood
113	AA1242	Rust
116	AA1287	US Dark Green
117	AA1290	US Light Green
118	AA1300	US Tan
119	AA1314	Light Earth
120	AA1328	Light Green
121	AA1331	Pale Stone
140	AA1523	Gull Grey
144	AA1568	Intermediate Blue
145	AA1571	Medium Grey
147	AA1599	Light Grey
148	AA1609	Radome Tan
149	AA1612	Dark Green
150	AA1626	Forest Green
153	AA1660	Insignia Red
154	AA1674	Insignia Yellow
155	AA1688	Olive Drab
159	AA1729	Khaki Drab
160	AA1732	German Camouflage Red Brown
173	AA0173	Track Colour
186	AA6224	Brown
224	AA7224	Dark Slate Grey
225	AA7225	Middle Stone
226	AA7226	Interior Green
230	AA1822	PRU Blue
234	AA0234	Dark Flesh
240	AA2240	RLM 02 Grau
241	AA2241	RLM 70 Schwartzgrün
242	AA2242	RLM 71 Dunkelgrün
243	AA2243	RLM 72 Grün
244	AA2244	RLM 73 Grün
245	AA2245	RLM 74 Graugrün
246	AA2246	RLM 75 Grauviolett
247	AA2247	RLM 76 Lichtblau
248	AA2248	RLM 78 Himmelblau
249	AA2249	RLM 79 Sandgelb
251	AA2251	RLM 81 Dunkelbraun
252	AA2252	RLM 82 Olivgrün
253	AA2253	RLM 83 Dunkel-Grün

Humbrol enamel paint has been the modeller's standard for decades. This superb paint can also be used as an art and craft paint on many different surfaces, both indoors and outdoors.

Please visit www.airfix.com/catalogue2019 to locate your nearest Humbrol stockist

Satin Colours 14ml

No.	Code	Name
71	AA0789	Oak
85	AA0936	Coal Black
123	AA1359	Extra Dark Sea Grey
125	AA1376	US Dark Grey
126	AA1393	US Medium Grey
127	AA1403	US Ghost Grey
128	AA1417	US Compass Grey
129	AA1420	US Gull Grey
130	AA1434	White
131	AA1448	Mid Green
132	AA1451	Red
133	AA1465	Brown
135	AA1482	Varnish
163	AA1777	Dark Green
164	AA1780	Dark Sea Grey
165	AA1794	Medium Sea Grey
166	AA1804	Light Aircraft Grey
168	AA1821	Hemp
174	AA1897	Signal Red
195	AA6330	Dark Green
196	AA6344	Light Grey

Gloss Colours 14ml

No.	Code	Name
2	AA0028 14ml / AQ0037 50ml	Emerald*
3	AA0031 14ml / AQ0040 50ml	Brunswick Green*
5	AA0059	Dark Admiralty
7	AA0076	Light Buff
9	AA0103	Tan
10	AA0117	Service Brown
14	AA0151 14ml / AQ0160 50ml	French Blue*
15	AA0165 14ml / AQ0174 50ml	Midnight Blue*
18	AA0196 14ml	Orange
19	AA0206 14ml / AQ0215 50ml	Bright Red*
20	AA0223 14ml / AQ0229 50ml	Crimson*
21	AA0237 14ml / AQ0232 50ml	Black*
22	AA0240 14ml / AQ0246 50ml	White*
35	AA0388 14ml / AQ0397 50ml	Varnish*
38	AA0415	Lime
40	AA0432	Pale Grey
41	AA0446	Ivory
47	AA0518	Sea Blue
48	AA0521	Mediterranean Blue
68	AA0758	Purple
69	AA0761 14ml / AQ0770 50ml	Yellow*
200	AA6389	Pink
208	AA7081	Fluorescent Signal Green
209	AA7105	Fluorescent Fire Orange
220	AA6608	Italian Red
238	AA0238	Arrow Red
239	AA0239	British Racing Green

*Also available in 50ml (No.2) tinlets.

Metallic Colours 14ml

No.	Code	Name
11	AA0120 14ml / AQ0126 50ml	Silver*
12	AA0134	Copper
16	AA0179 14ml / AQ0188 50ml	Gold*
50	AA0549	Green Mist
51	AA0552	Sunset Red
52	AA0566	Baltic Blue
53	AA0583	Gunmetal
54	AA0597	Brass
55	AA0607	Bronze
56	AA0610	Aluminium
171	AA1852	Antique Bronze
191	AA6272	Chrome Silver
201	AA6392	Metallic Black
222	AA7222	Moonlight Blue

Metalcote Colours 14ml

No.	Code	Name
27001	AC5008	Aluminium
27002	AC5011	Polished Aluminium
27003	AC5025	Polished Steel
27004	AC5039	Gunmetal

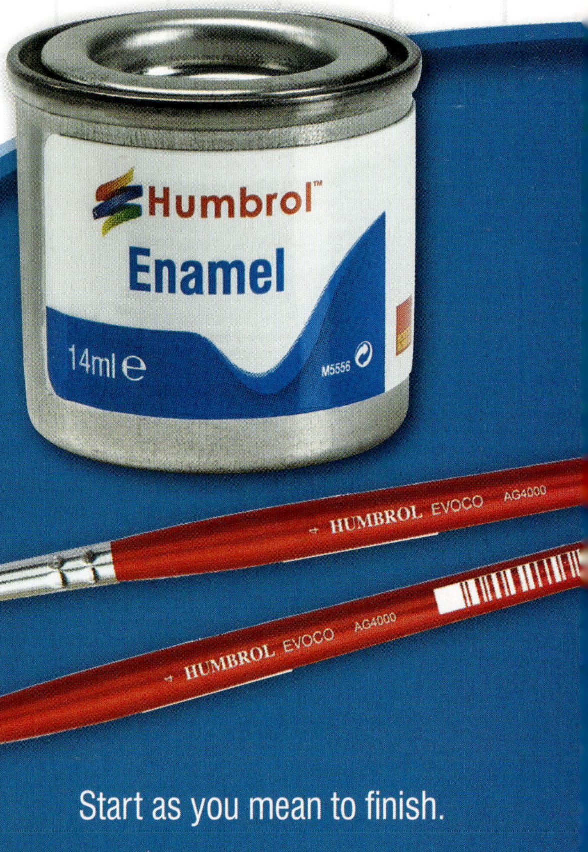

Start as you mean to finish.

www.humbrol.com

100 YEARS OF Humbrol™ Acrylic Paints

Matt Colours 14ml

No.	Code	Name
1	AB0001	Grey Primer
24	AB0024	Trainer Yellow
25	AB0025	Blue
26	AB0026	Khaki
27	AB0027	Sea Grey
29	AB0029	Dark Earth
30	AB0030	Dark Green
32	AB0032	Dark Grey
33	AB0033	Black
34	AB0034	White
49	AB0049	Varnish
60	AB0060	Scarlet
61	AB0061	Flesh
62	AB0062	Leather
63	AB0063	Sand
64	AB0064	Light Grey
65	AB0065	Aircraft Blue
67	AB0067	Tank Grey
78	AB0078	Cockpit Green
83	AB0083	Ochre
86	AB0086	Light Olive
87	AB0087	Steel Grey
93	AB0093	Desert Yellow
94	AB0094	Brown Yellow
99	AB0099	Lemon
102	AB0102	Army Green
103	AB0103	Cream
106	AB0106	Ocean Grey
110	AB0110	Natural Wood
117	AB0117	US Light Green
118	AB0118	US Tan
154	AB0154	Insignia Yellow
155	AB0155	Olive Drab
160	AB0160	German Camouflage Red Brown
186	AB0186	Brown
226	AB0226	Interior Green
230	AB0230	PRU Blue
240	AB0240	RLM 02 Grau
241	AB0241	RLM 70 Schwartzgrün
242	AB0242	RLM 71 Dunkelgrün
243	AB0243	RLM 72 Grün
244	AB0244	RLM 73 Grün
245	AB0245	RLM 74 Graugrün
246	AB0246	RLM 75 Grauviolett
247	AB0247	RLM 76 Lichtblau
248	AB0248	RLM 78 Himmelblau
249	AB0249	RLM 79 Sandgelb
251	AB0251	RLM 81 Dunkelbraun
252	AB0252	RLM 82 Olivgrün
253	AB0253	RLM83 Dunkel-Grün

Satin Colours 14ml

No.	Code	Name
71	AB0071	Oak
85	AB0085	Coal Black
123	AB0123	Extra Dark Sea Grey
127	AB0127	US Ghost Grey
130	AB0130	White
135	AB0135	Varnish
156	AB0156	Dark Camouflage Grey
163	AB0163	Dark Green
164	AB0164	Dark Sea Grey
165	AB0165	Medium Sea Grey
167	AB0167	RAF Barley Grey
168	AB0168	Hemp
174	AB0174	Signal Red

With the Humbrol Acrylic range having grown to over 100 colours, it will satisfy almost every modeller's needs. Being water-based it's easy to apply both by brush, which can then be cleaned with water, or by airbrush, thinned with water or a small amount of Acrylic Thinners, depending on personal preference. The paint is hard wearing and can be used on most surfaces, both indoors and outdoors.

Please visit www.airfix.com/catalogue2019 to locate your nearest Humbrol stockist

Gloss Colours 14ml

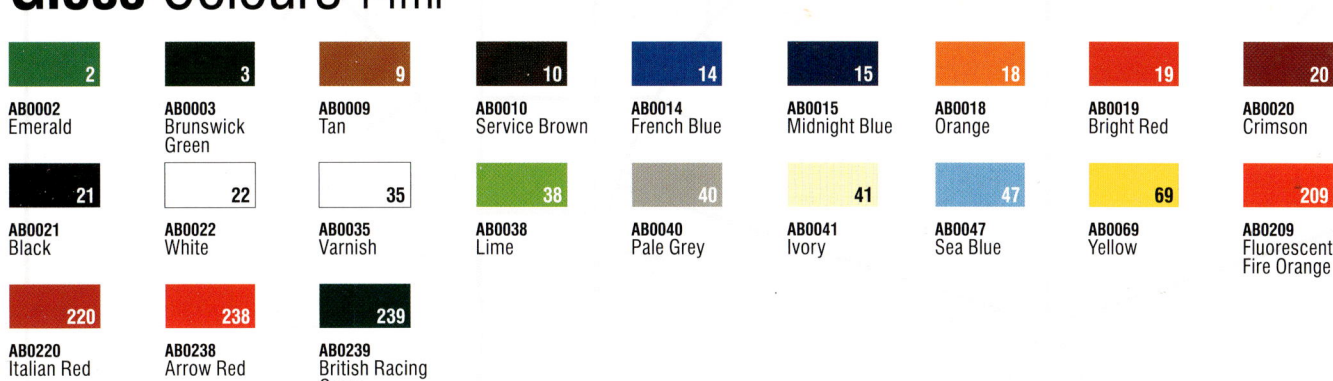

Code	Number	Name
AB0002	2	Emerald
AB0003	3	Brunswick Green
AB0009	9	Tan
AB0010	10	Service Brown
AB0014	14	French Blue
AB0015	15	Midnight Blue
AB0018	18	Orange
AB0019	19	Bright Red
AB0020	20	Crimson
AB0021	21	Black
AB0022	22	White
AB0035	35	Varnish
AB0038	38	Lime
AB0040	40	Pale Grey
AB0041	41	Ivory
AB0047	47	Sea Blue
AB0069	69	Yellow
AB0209	209	Fluorescent Fire Orange
AB0220	220	Italian Red
AB0238	238	Arrow Red
AB0239	239	British Racing Green

Metallic Colours 14ml

Code	Number	Name
AB0011	11	Silver
AB0012	12	Copper
AB0016	16	Gold
AB0052	52	Baltic Blue
AB0053	53	Gunmetal
AB0056	56	Aluminium
AB0171	171	Antique Bronze
AB0191	191	Chrome Silver

Matt Rail Colours 14ml

The Humbrol acrylic range of popular railway colours have been developed to suit many variations on the UK rail network of multiple eras. These paints are also ideally suited for weathering, dry brushing and re-touching, taking your model railways hobby to a new level.

Code	RC Number	Name
AB2401	RC401	Dirty Black
AB2403	RC403	Crimson Lake
AB2404	RC404	Garter Blue
AB2405	RC405	GWR/BR Green
AB2406	RC406	Buffer Beam Red
AB2408	RC408	Apple Green
AB2409	RC409	Malachite Green
AB2410	RC410	Maunsell Green
AB2411	RC411	Diesel Blue
AB2412	RC412	BR Coach Roof Grey
AB2413	RC413	Engineers Grey
AB2414	RC414	Executive Dark Grey
AB2415	RC415	Pullman Umber Brown
AB2416	RC416	Pullman Cream
AB2418	RC418	EWS Red
AB2419	RC419	EWS Yellow
AB2420	RC420	Orange Lining
AB2421	RC421	Virgin Red
AB2422	RC422	Intercity Grey
AB2423	RC423	Carmine
AB2424	RC424	BR Cream

Start as you mean to finish.

www.humbrol.com

100 YEARS OF Humbrol™ Paint & Brush Sets

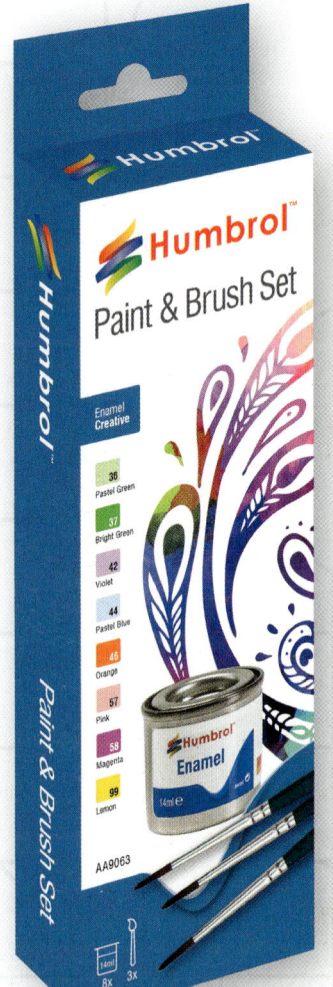

Enamel Creative
Paint and Brush Set

3 brushes
36 Pastel Green
37 Bright Green
42 Violet
44 Pastel Blue
46 Orange
57 Pink
58 Magenta
99 Lemon
AA9063

Enamel Metallic
Paint and Brush Set

3 brushes
11 Silver
16 Gold
52 Baltic Blue
53 Gunmetal
54 Brass
55 Bronze
56 Aluminium
201 Black
AA9062

Enamel Matt
Paint and Brush Set

3 brushes
24 Yellow
25 Blue
29 Dark Earth
30 Dark Green
33 Black
34 White
60 Scarlet
61 Flesh
AA9061

See pages 124 through 127 for acrylic and enamel colour charts

Please visit www.airfix.com/catalogue2019 to locate your nearest Humbrol stockist

The Paint & Brush Sets here are for those wanting a good concise selection of paints and brushes in one easy purchase. These sets are particularly helpful for anyone using these excellent paints for non-plastic modelling hobbies and tasks.

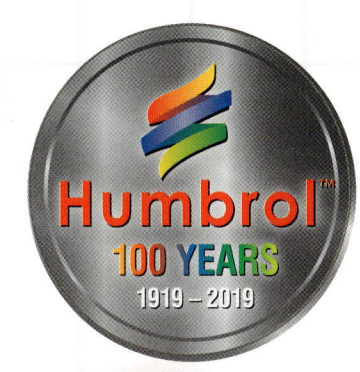

Humbrol
100 YEARS
1919 – 2019

Enamel Gloss
Paint and Brush Set

3 brushes
1 Grey Primer
2 Emerald
14 French Blue
18 Orange
19 Bright Red
21 Black
22 White
69 Yellow
AA9060

Acrylic Scenic
Paint and Brush Set

3 brushes
63 Sand
70 Brick Red
91 Black Green
99 Lemon
113 Rust
117 Light Green
186 Brown
226 Green
ABA9061

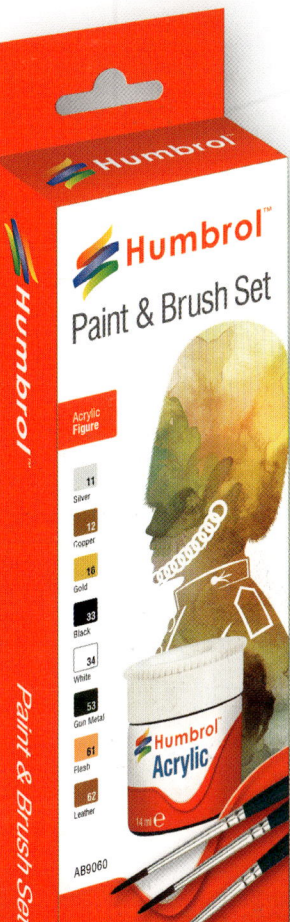

Acrylic Figure
Paint and Brush Set

3 brushes
11 Silver
12 Copper
16 Gold
33 Black
34 White
53 Gun Metal
61 Flesh
62 Leather
AB9060

A great gift idea!
The perfect package for any craft project

Start as you mean to finish.

www.humbrol.com

100 YEARS OF Humbrol™ Spray Paints

A fast drying acrylic-based paint for use not only on plastic kits, but also on other substrates including, polycarbonate, wood, glass, ceramics, metal, card and many more craft and DIY uses.

Matt Colours 150ml

No.	Code	Name
1	AD6001	Grey Primer
27	AD6027	Sea Grey
29	AD6029	Dark Earth
30	AD6030	Dark Green
33	AD6033	Black
34	AD6034	White
63	AD6063	Sand
64	AD6064	Light Grey
67	AD6067	Tank Grey
80	AD6080	Grass Green
86	AD6086	Light Olive
90	AD6090	Beige Green
93	AD6093	Desert Yellow
155	AD6155	Olive Drab
237	AD6237	Desert Tan

Gloss Colours 150ml

No.	Code	Name
3	AD6003	Brunswick Green
14	AD6014	French Blue
15	AD6015	Midnight Blue
18	AD6018	Orange
19	AD6019	Bright Red
21	AD6021	Black
22	AD6022	White
38	AD6038	Lime
68	AD6068	Purple
69	AD6069	Yellow
220	AD6220	Italian Red

Metallic Colours 150ml

No.	Code	Name
11	AD6011	Silver
12	AD7704	Copper
16	AD6016	Gold
53	AD6053	Gunmetal
54	AD6054	Brass
56	AD6056	Aluminium
191	AD6191	Chrome Silver

Satin Colours 150ml

No.	Code	Name
85	AD6085	Black
163	AD6163	Dark Green
165	AD6165	Medium Sea Grey

Fluorescent Colours 150ml

Code	Name
AD6202	Pink
AD6210	Blue

Humbrol™ Glass Etch Spray

Glass Etch 150ml

Use Humbrol Glass Etch to transform mirrors, interior doors and windows. Used in conjunction with stencils, a wide range of designer effects can be created.

Code	Name
AD7701	Glass Etch Pink
AD7702	Glass Etch Blue
AD7703	Glass Etch Green

Please visit www.airfix.com/catalogue2019 to locate your nearest Humbrol stockist

100 YEARS OF Humbrol™ Spray Paints

Multi-Effect Sprays 150ml

Ideal for a wide range of uses; plastic kits, slot cars, remote control subjects, along with decorative and craft projects. Humbrol Multi-Effect Sprays must be applied on a black undercoat/surface. To achieve optimum durability, we also recommend using Humbrol acrylic varnish.

AD6211 Gold	AD6212 Red	AD6212 Blue	AD6214 Green	AD6215 Violet

Metalcote Colours 150ml

Humbrol Metalcotes have been designed to give the appearance of polished metals. Once dry, polish with a soft cloth until you reach the desired look.

27002 AD6995 Polished Aluminium	27003 AD6996 Polished Steel

Humbrol™ Varnish Spray

Acrylic Varnish 150ml

Suitable for applying over acrylic paint.

35 AD6035 Gloss Varnish	49 AD6049 Matt Varnish	135 AD6135 Satin Varnish

Enamel Varnish 150ml

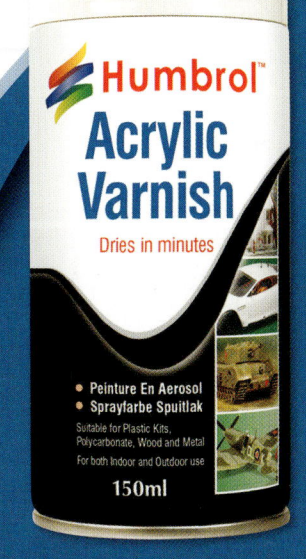

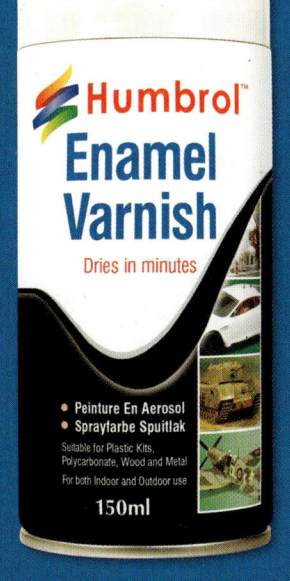

35 AD6997 Gloss Varnish	49 AD6998 Matt Varnish	135 AD6999 Satin Varnish

www.humbrol.com

100 YEARS OF Humbrol™ Adhesives & Fillers

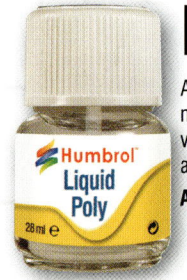

Liquid Poly
A solvent-based cement suitable for plastic model kits only. The product is a lower viscosity version of Polycement to enable application by brush

AE2500 28ml bottle

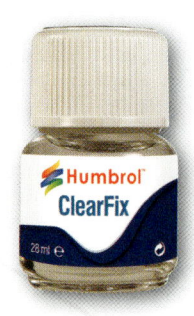

Clearfix
A solvent-based polymer solution for use as an adhesive on clear plastic parts without the risk of the 'frosting' effect sometimes seen using traditional glues.
It can also be used for making small windows or translucent areas of 3mm or less.

AC5708 28ml bottle

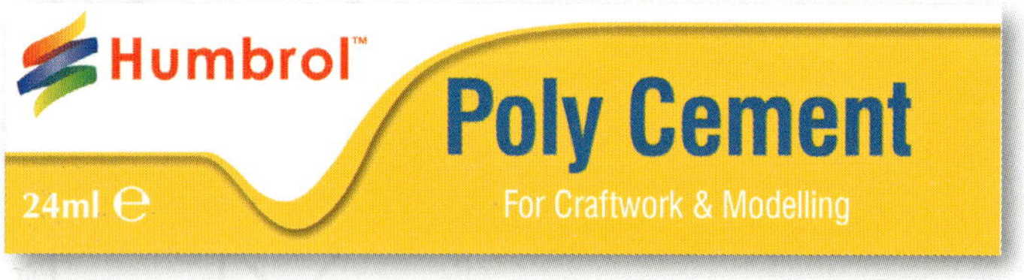

Poly Cement
A solvent-based cement suitable for plastic model kits only.

AE4021 12ml medium (tube)
AE4422 24ml large (tube)

Precision Poly Cement
A solvent-based cement suitable for plastic model kits only.
Its viscosity is low to enable precision delivery of fine amounts of cement

AE2720 20ml precision poly dispenser

Balsa Cement
A quick-drying transparent cement for balsa, soft woods and cork.

AE0603 24ml (tube)

Model Filler
A fine grade model filler which can be sanded, filed and painted once dry.

AE3016 31ml (tube)

Humbrol 100 YEARS 1919 – 2019

Turn your model kit into a masterpiece!

Please visit www.airfix.com/catalogue2019 to locate your nearest Humbrol stockist

100 YEARS OF Humbrol™ Coatings & Thinners

Enamel Thinners

Used to thin down Humbrol Enamel paints most commonly for airbrushing. Can also be used to thin down other solvent based products such as Enamel Washes, Modelcotes and Model Filler.

AC7501 28ml bottle
AC7430 125ml bottle

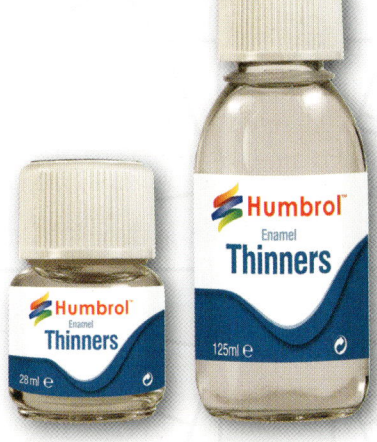

Acrylic Thinners

Humbrol Acrylic Thinners has been especially formulated to enhance the quality and usability of Humbrol Acrylic paint when brushing and airbrushing. The Thinners includes a retardant which reduces the drying rate and greatly improves the use of Acrylic paint when airbrushing. Can also be used to clean your brushes after use with Acrylic paint.

AC7433 125ml bottle

Clear

These thin, water-based self-levelling varnishes are ideal for brush and airbrush. You have the option of three finishes, these are; Gloss, Matt or Satin with a higher level of any achieved by applying further thin coats.

AC7431 Gloss 125ml bottle
AC7434 Matt 125ml bottle
AC7435 Satin 125ml bottle

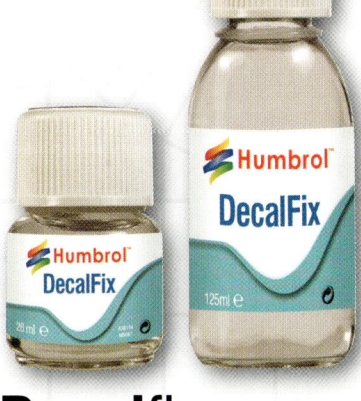

Decalfix

A water based solution that softens decals and secures them in place by drawing the decal around and in any panel lines. Decals are permanent once dry.

AC6134 28ml bottle
AC7432 125ml bottle

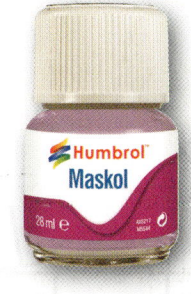

Maskol

A rubber solution that can be applied to surfaces to prevent them from being painted. When the paint has dried the Maskol can simply be peeled off.

AC5217 28ml bottle

Gloss Cote

A solvent-based varnish that goes on clear and dries clear, overcoming the yellowing effect associated with traditional varnishes. The product dries to a smooth, high-sheen gloss finish.

AC5501 28ml bottle

Satin Cote

A solvent-based varnish that goes on clear and dries clear, overcoming the yellowing effect associated with traditional varnishes. The product dries to a smooth, mid-sheen satin/eggshell finish.

AC5401 28ml bottle

Matt Cote

A solvent-based varnish that goes on clear and dries clear, overcoming the yellowing effect associated with traditional varnishes. The product dries to a smooth, low-sheen matt finish.

AC5601 28ml bottle

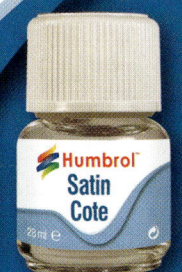

www.humbrol.com

100 YEARS OF Humbrol™

Weathering Powders 28ml

Humbrol Weathering Powders are a versatile means of adding realistic weathering effects to your models, figures and dioramas. They can be mixed to create different shades, enabling a full range of finishes including dust, mud, soot, rust and many more.

AV0001	Black
AV0002	White
AV0003	Sand
AV0004	Smoke
AV0005	Chrome Oxide Green
AV0006	Iron Oxide
AV0007	Dark Earth
AV0008	Rust

Enamel Washes 28ml

Enhance your models with the Humbrol Enamel Washes range, designed for a wide range of uses they are easy to use and very durable.

AV0201	Black
AV0202	White
AV0203	Dark Green
AV0204	Dark Grey
AV0205	Dark Brown
AV0206	Blue Grey
AV0207	Sand
AV0208	Dust
AV0209	Oil Stain
AV0210	Rust

Please visit www.airfix.com/catalogue2019 to locate your nearest Humbrol stockist

100 YEARS OF Humbrol™ Work Station
a MUST for all modellers!

The Humbrol Work Station has many features:

- Double depth sections for holding 9 x 14ml Humbrol Enamel or Acrylic pots, or 3ml Humbrol Acrylic pots
- Double depth water cup holders, allow the modeller to place Humbrol 28ml products, such as; matt, satin & gloss cotes, Decalfix, Maskol, Clearfix, Thinners and Liquid Poly
- Designed to fit the new Humbrol A4 Cutting mat within the working area
- Two mixing areas either side of the Cutting Mat
- Easy to hold handles either side of the Work Station
- Rubber feet, which allows the modeller to place on a flat surface
- A4 Instruction sheet holder
- Brush and tool holders.

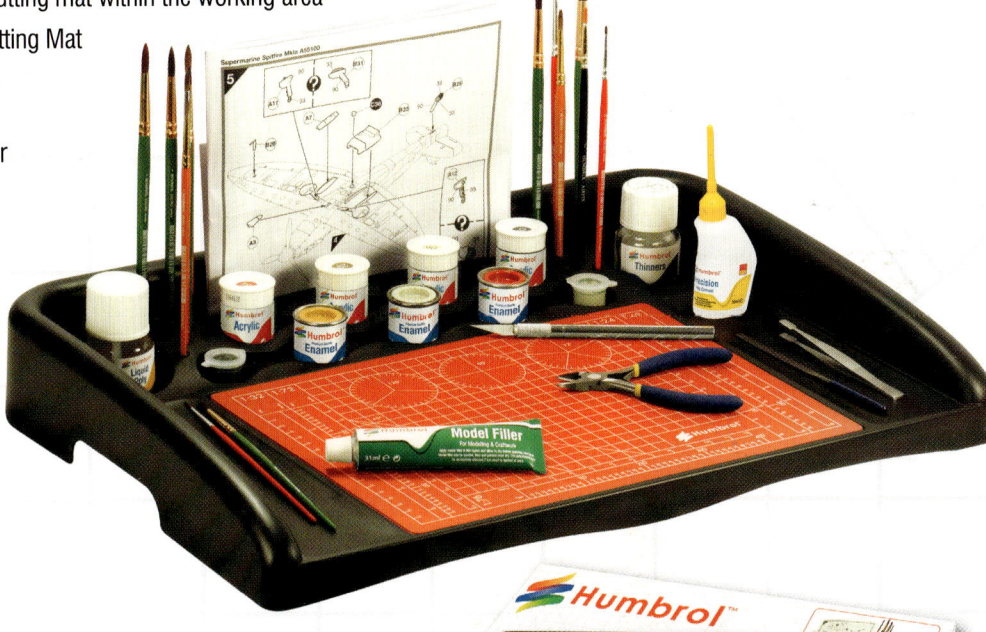

The Humbrol Work Station is manufactured from a tough and durable material that can't be melted by Humbrol Poly Cement.

AG9156

Please Note: Paints, brushes and other Humbrol products shown are not included.

Humbrol™ Colour Chart

This year we've also updated our Enamel Paint and Conversion Chart which provides a great overview of the colours on offer and an in-depth cross reference chart with other popular paint brands.

P1158 Humbrol Enamel Paint and Conversion Chart

www.humbrol.com

100 YEARS OF Humbrol™ Brushes

Coloro Brushes

The Coloro range of brushes are perfectly suited for all paint types, but are particularly good when used in conjunction with the new Humbrol Acrylic Paint. Made from man-made fibre

Size 00 – **AG4030**
Size 0 – **AG4000**
Size 1 – **AG4001**
Size 2 – **AG4002**
Size 4 – **AG4004**

Coloro pack.
Size 00, 1, 4, 8 – **AG4050**

Evoco Brushes

Made from natural hair, Evoco brushes are the perfect "all-round" brush for many model and hobby uses, keeping their shape and quality long after their first use.

Size 000 – **AG4131**
Size 0 – **AG4100**
Size 2 – **AG4102**
Size 4 – **AG4104**
Size 6 – **AG4106**
Size 8 – **AG4108**

Evoco pack.
Size 0, 2, 4, 6 – **AG4150**

Palpo Brushes

The Palpo natural sable hair brushes are the ultimate modelling brush, keeping their points and shape to allow for accurate and detailed painting, particularly figure work.

Size 00000 – **AG4233**
Size 000 – **AG4231**
Size 0 – **AG4200**

Palpo pack.
Size 000, 0, 2, 4 – **AG4250**

Detail Brushes

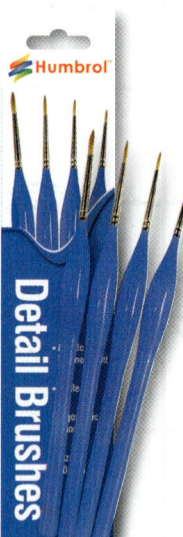

These ultra fine sable hair brushes are ideal for painting small detailed areas on your models/figures. The easy grip ergonomic handles make them a pleasure to use for short or long periods of time.

Suitable for Enamel and Acrylic paints.

Detail pack.
Size 00, 0, 1, 2 – **AG4304**

Flat Brushes

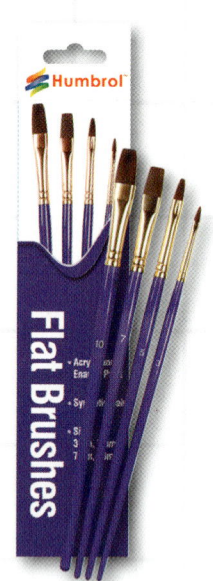

Made from high quality soft synthetic hair, the Flat Brush pack is perfect for creating a smooth professional finish. Ideal for painting large surface areas, weathering, adding washes and helping to apply decals.

Suitable for Enamel and Acrylic paints.

Flat pack.
Size 3, 5, 7, 10 – **AG4305**

Stipple Brushes

The Stipple Brushes have been designed with heavy dry brushing and weathering in mind. Made from a tough natural hair, which is perfect when adding those finishing touches when bringing your models to life.

Suitable for Enamel and Acrylic paints, as well as Weathering Powder.

Stipple pack.
Size 3, 5, 7, 10 – **AG4306**

Top tips on how to use Humbrol products are available at **www.Humbrol.com**. You can also see the products in action on the Official Humbrol YouTube Channel, **www.youtube.com/Humbrol**

Please visit **www.airfix.com/catalogue2019** to locate your nearest Humbrol stockist

100 YEARS OF Humbrol™ Tool Sets & Mats

Tool Sets

The kit modeller's tool set
Specifically designed for the Airfix and plastic kit modeller – sprue clippers, tweezers, needle file and knife; all designed for making the perfect model.
AG9150 – Small
AG9159 – Medium

A3 Cutting Mat
A4 Cutting Mat

The kit modeller's mat
The "Kit Modellers" Cutting Mat is a self-sealing cutting mat with graphics and scale markings to suit all categories of plastic modelling.
A3 AG9157
A4 AG9155

Humbrol™ Airbrushes

All Purpose Airbrush

A great beginners airbrush to introduce the skill of airbrushing at a great value price. Use with cans of Humbrol Airbrush Propellant or a compressor. All purpose airbrush (blister)
AG5107

Airbrush Powerpack

Airbrush Powerpack
Airbrush powerpack 400ml
AV6941

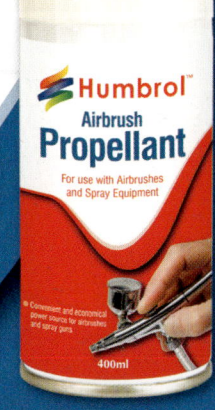

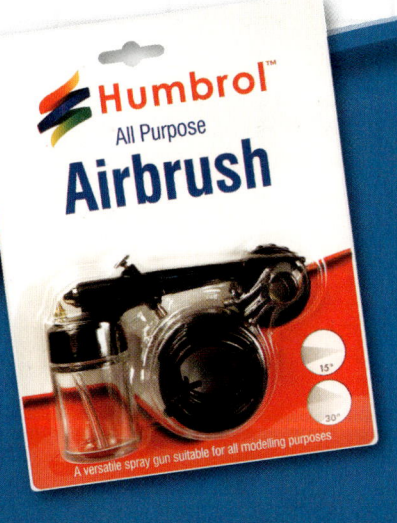

The full range of accessories is designed to meet every modeller's needs. Whether it is your first ever model build or your collection is in to the hundreds these products will help you get the most out of your build.

www.humbrol.com

HORNBY® SKALE SCENICS

100 YEARS OF Humbrol™

00 Gauge Model Railway Scenics

Trains, tracks and buildings make a railway layout, but to make a model railway a landscape needs to be created, adding realism and atmosphere to the miniature world.

By adding trees, bushes, grass and stone, scenery is brought to life by adding texture, colour, scale and depth to even the smallest of layouts. Research, planning and preparation is essential for successful landscape modelling, whether it is a scree covered Highland scene or a gentle rolling wooded landscape, so the SkaleScenic range covers the essential elements needed.

Scatter and ballast can be used as single colour cover, or mixed to add tone, while flock adds texture to ground cover. Detailing elements can then be added, with grasses and bushes adding depth and trees adding scale, as individual items, in small groups, or in bulk to represent woodland and forests.

Product	Size	Pack	Code
Fruit Trees	80mm	Three per pack	R7202
Maple Trees	90mm	Three per pack	R7203
Beech Trees	130mm	Two per pack	R7204
Birch Trees	45mm	Three per pack	R7205
Large Fir Trees	80-120mm	Four per pack	R7206
Small Fir Trees	40-80mm	Four per pack	R7207
Bushes	30-40mm	Five per pack	R7208
Oak Tree	150mm	Single item	R7209
Lime Tree	185mm	Single item	R7210
Horse Chestnut Tree	190mm	Single item	R7211
'Hobby' Deciduous Trees	50-90mm	Twenty per pack	R7198
'Hobby' Fir Trees	50-140mm	Twenty per pack	R7199
'Hobby' Mixed (Deciduous and Fir) Trees	50-140mm	Twenty per pack	R7201

Please visit www.airfix.com/catalogue2019 to locate your nearest Humbrol stockist

Fruit Tree	Apple Tree (with Fruit)	Pear Tree
75mm | Single item — R7212	75mm | Single item — R7213	75mm | Single item — R7214

Birch Tree	Rowan Tree (with Berries)	Acacia Tree
115mm | Single item — R7215	115mm | Single item — R7216	150mm | Single item — R7217

Tree (with Circular Bench)	Beech Tree	Oak Tree
115mm | Single item — R7218	130mm | Single item — R7219	160mm | Single item — R7220

Lime Tree	Horse-Chestnut Tree	Lime Tree
185mm | Single item — R7221	195mm | Single item — R7222	185mm | Single item — R7223

Tree (with Tree House)	Medium Nordic Fir Tree	Large Nordic Fir Tree
150mm | Single item — R7224	120mm | Single item — R7225	145mm | Single item — R7226

Medium Pine Tree	Large Pine Tree
120mm | Single item — R7227	150mm | Single item — R7228

Handmade for finer quality, the SkaleScenics Profi Tree range will bring added scenic detail to any model railway or diorama.

The trunks of the trees are painted by hand so that no shining plastic surfaces are left visible and to give more volume, all of the branches are covered with fine wool before they are flocked. This mimics the leaf shapes and colours of a real tree and, as in nature, only the fine branches of the PROFI trees have leaves, so this is replicated with our range.

www.humbrol.com

Ballast

Brown	Grey	Limestone	Granite	Basaltic Rock
Weight 250g — R7164	Weight 250g — R7165	Weight 250g — R7166	Weight 250g — R7167	Weight 250g — R7168

Gneiss	Coal
Weight 250g — R7169	Weight 250g — R7170

Note: To cover an area of 1m^2 you will need approximately 100 g scatter material and 500g of Grass Glue.

Scatter

Flower Meadow	Light Green	Medium Green	Dark Green	Brown
Weight 42g — R7171	Weight 42g — R7172	Weight 42g — R7173	Weight 42g — R7176	Weight 42g — R7174

Grey
Weight 42g — R7175

Flockage and Flock

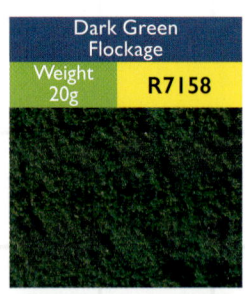

Bright Green Flockage	Medium Green Flockage	Dark Green Flockage	Medium Brown Flockage	Dark Brown Flockage
Weight 20g — R7156	Weight 20g — R7157	Weight 20g — R7158	Weight 20g — R7159	Weight 20g — R7160

Bright Green Flock	Medium Green Flock	Dark Green Flock
Weight 20g — R7161	Weight 20g — R7162	Weight 20g — R7163

Humbrol™ 100 YEARS 1919 – 2019

Please visit www.airfix.com/catalogue2019 to locate your nearest Humbrol stockist

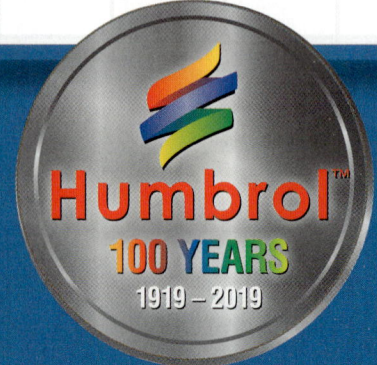

Static Grass

Spring Meadow, 2.5mm	Grass Meadow, 2.5mm	Ornamental Lawn, 2.5mm	Mixed Summer, 2.5mm	Alpine Meadow (with Boulders), 2.5mm
Weight 20g — R7177	Weight 20g — R7178	Weight 20g — R7179	Weight 20g — R7180	Weight 20g — R7181

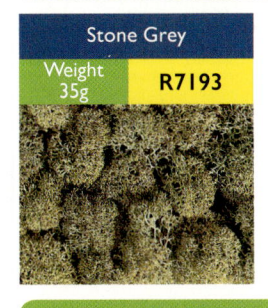

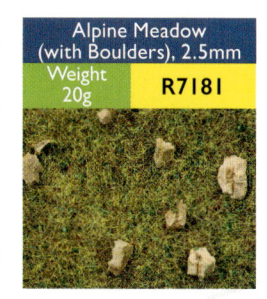

Lichen

Stone Grey	Green Mix	Autumn Mix	Large Green Mix	Large Autumn Mix
Weight 35g — R7193	Weight 35g — R7194	Weight 35g — R7196	Weight 75g — R7195	Weight 75g — R7197

Foliage

Light Green	Dark Green	Olive Green	Wild Grass (Light Green)	Wild Grass (Dark Green)
Covering 20x23cm — R7184	Covering 20x23cm — R7185	Covering 20x23cm — R7186	Covering 20x23cm — R7187	Covering 20x23cm — R7188

Yellow Green Meadow	Middle Green Meadow	Leafy - Middle Green	Leafy - Dark Green
Covering 20x23cm — R7189	Covering 20x23cm — R7190	Covering 20x23cm — R7191	Covering 20x23cm — R7192

Accessories

Grass Glue	Static Grass Puffer Bottle
Weight 250g — R7183	Use with R7183 to apply Static Grasses — R7182

www.humbrol.com

100 YEARS OF Humbrol™ Product Chart

Paint Products	Usage	Substrate
Enamel Paint	A solvent-based, fast-dry paint developed for use on plastic model kits but which can also be used on other substrates (see right). Matt, Satin, Gloss, Metallic, Metalcote and Clear finishes are available.	A wide range of surfaces including most plastics, wood, glass, ceramics, metal, cardboard, sealed plaster, sealed hardboard and many more.
Acrylic Paint	A water-based, fast dry paint developed for use on plastic model kits but which can also be used on other substrates. Matt, Satin, Gloss, Metallic and Clear finishes are available.	A wide range of surfaces including most plastics, wood, glass, ceramics, metal, cardboard, sealed plaster, sealed hardboard and many more.
Acrylic Spray	A solvent-based, fast-dry paint developed for use on plastic model kits but which can also be used on other substrates (see right). Matt, Satin, Gloss, Metallic and Clear finishes are available.	A wide range of surfaces including most plastics, wood, glass, ceramics, metal, cardboard, sealed plaster, sealed hardboard and many more.
Varnish Spray	Protects and creates a desired finish: Matt, Satin & Gloss.	Overcoat for the applicable paint type.
Metal Cote Spray	Creates a polished look once dry and buffed.	A wide range of surfaces including most plastics, wood, glass, ceramics, metal, cardboard, sealed plaster, sealed hardboard and many more.
Weathering Powder	Used to create realistic weathered effects.	Weathering Powder can be applied to most substrates depending on the method. For full details, please visit the Humbrol website.
Enamel Wash	Used to create realistic weathered, oiled and grime effects on scale models.	Humbrol Enamel Washes can be applied to most substrates depending on the method. For full details, please visit the Humbrol website.

Glues	Usage	Substrate
Poly Cement	A solvent-based cement suitable for plastic model kits only.	Common plastics used to manufacture model kits including polystyrene and ABS. The product works by melting the plastic on application and 'welding' two glued pieces of plastic together to form a strong bond.
Model Filler	Fills hairline cracks and gaps between plastic parts. The product can be sanded when fully dry using a fine grade of sandpaper and painted.	Plastic model kits.
Balsa Cement	A quick-drying transparent cement for balsa, other soft woods and cork.	Balsa, other soft woods and cork.

Detail Application	Usage	Substrate
Clearfix	A solvent-based polymer solution for use as an adhesive on clear plastic parts without the risk of the 'frosting' effect sometimes seen using traditional glues and for making small windows or translucent areas of 3mm or less.	Common plastics used to manufacture model kits including polystyrene and ABS.
Decalfix	A water-based solution for softening decals and securing them into position.	Decals are usually applied onto painted surfaces. Care should be taken to avoid 'silvering' over matt paints.
Maskol	A rubber solution that can be applied to surfaces to prevent them being painted. When the paint has dried the Maskol can be simply peeled off.	Common plastics used to manufacture model kits including polystyrene and ABS and a wide variety of other applications including glass.
Enamel Thinner	Thinning down of solvent-based enamel paints, most commonly for airbrushing.	Enamel paint and other Humbrol solvent based products.
Acrylic Thinner	Thinning down of Humbrol Acrylic paints, most commonly for airbrushing.	Acrylic paint.

Finishing	Usage	Substrate
Mattcote/Satincote/Glosscote	A solvent-based varnish that goes on clear and dries clear, overcoming the yellowing effect associated with traditional varnishes. The product dries to a smooth, low-sheen matt finish.	Common plastics used to manufacture model kits including polystyrene and ABS, as well as MDF. Matt cote is usually applied as the final coat to a fully painted and decaled model.
Clear	A water soluble, self-levelling medium in either gloss, matt or satin that can be used to prepare surfaces. Gloss varnish can be used to prepare surfaces for decals and to improve the appearance of clear parts.	Humbrol Enamel and Acrylic Paint.

Please visit www.airfix.com/catalogue2019 to locate your nearest Humbrol stockist